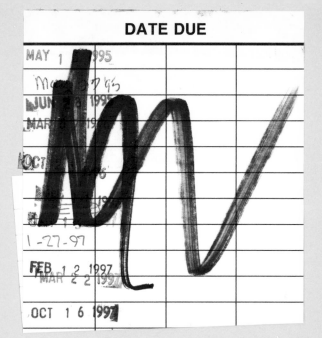

50 CHARACTER DOLLS

to make at home

Paul Moran

50
CHARACTER
DOLLS

to make at home

A DAVID & CHARLES CRAFT BOOK

Many thanks to Kym Wagner, editor of *Popular Crafts*, for letting me reproduce the Downhill Skier and Eastern Princess dolls, which first appeared in her pages.

British Library Cataloguing in Publication Data
Moran, Paul
  50 Character dolls to make at home: full-size patterns for
  50 delightful dolls. – (A David & Charles craft book).
  1. Dolls. Making
  I. Title
  745.59221

  ISBN 0-17-539787-7

Typeset by Typesetters (Birmingham) Limited, Smethwick, West Midlands
and printed in Italy
  by **OFSA** S.p.A.
for David & Charles Publishers plc
Brunel House Newton Abbot Devon

Distributed in the United States by
Sterling Publishing Co. Inc.
387 Park Avenue South, New York, NY 10016–8810

Contents

Introduction

For centuries people have made cloth dolls, from the earliest primitive dolls to the more elaborate porcelain dolls adopted by the Victorians; over recent years, interest in doll collecting and making has soared.

This book contains fifty dolls all made from the five basic body patterns given at the front of the book. Each body varies slightly in construction; there are dolls that stand on a base, more traditional rag dolls, large and small dolls with stockinette heads and even a fishy pattern to make two mermaids!

Each chapter has a theme: Seasonal Dolls, Beach Dolls, Costume Dolls, Shakespearean Dolls and finally a chapter with fairies and pixies galore.

Fabric dolls have an individual charm of their own and although specific fabric requirements are given for each doll, you can add personal touches with your own colour schemes and trimmings which are guaranteed to transform the simplest doll into a glittery fairy, witch, wizard or eastern princess. Each chapter also contains dolls for boys; including a pirate, space hero, santa, gnomes and leprechauns and others.

In this book you can escape into a land of make-believe where there is hopefully a doll to suit every taste, so welcome to the enchanting world of dollmaking!

The Land of the Little People: (from left) a chirpy Pixie; the Orange Fairy; a lively Leprechaun and a tired Gnome (see pages 143–59)

Guidelines and Hints

EQUIPMENT

SCISSORS

Try to use a good sharp pair of dressmaking scissors for cutting out large pieces of fabric. A pair of small embroidery scissors will be useful for cutting tiny pieces of fabric such as eyes. For cutting paper and card a pair of general purpose scissors is handy.

THREAD

When making up doll bodies try to use a strong thread. Even though some dolls may be made purely for decoration it is surprising how much they are handled!

White thread has been used to sew most of the lighter coloured fabrics, whilst black thread has been used for the darker colours; if you try to match up different coloured sewing thread for the clothes on each doll it will not only drive you to distraction but prove very expensive!

NEEDLES

You can buy a packet containing a selection of needles quite cheaply; medium needles are useful for general sewing, small needles for tiny pieces of fabric and long darning needles are essential to sew mouths and eyelashes. Fine beading needles are handy for sewing on sequins and beads although you will probably have to buy these separately.

GLUE

Use an all-purpose glue such as UHU which is very strong, sticks both fabric and card, is transparent and dries very quickly.

STUFFING

Spend a little more on a good-quality toy stuffing so that your doll will have a nice smooth finish when stuffed. Try to buy stuffing in bulk; this not only saves you money in the long run but also saves you from dashing out to the shops when you suddenly find that you have run out!

MATERIALS

CHOOSING FABRICS

The fabrics you choose to make a doll help to create a character and will decide whether the doll is a success or not. Try to choose a good-quality flesh calico with a close weave when making doll bodies, similarly a good-quality stretchy stockinette fabric will make life much easier when stuffing heads. Choosing fabrics for clothes is important too; try not to use fabrics with large prints or stripes since these will look out of scale on small dolls.

Some of the fabrics used for the more creative dolls need to be slightly more exotic; brocades, chiffons, satins and glittery fabrics help to achieve quite dramatic effects. You do not need to spend vast amounts of money, however; look out for bargains in your local fabric shops and department stores. Jumble sales and charity shops are an endless source of supply for fabrics; a tatty evening dress, old curtain or nightgown may look rather uninviting at first sight, but once washed and pressed they will look as good as new and you can simply cut the fabric you need from them. Sometimes trying to find the right fabric for the type of effect you want can be a problem, so try

to buy oddments of unusual fabrics as you see them and store them in a bag or box until required.

FELT

Always work with good-quality felt since a poor quality one will start to fray as soon as you begin stitching it and will ruin the appearance of your doll.

TRIMMINGS

To best effect, the trimmings you choose should complement the character and style of each doll.

Lace, ribbons, sequins, buttons and bows are all ways of trimming up a doll and all are widely available and come in a vast selection of colours. Sometimes, however, it may be difficult to find the exact shade you want so it is a good idea to buy the odd length of ribbon or braid as you see it and build up a collection in labelled bags or boxes to use as and when required.

As with fabrics, you do not need to spend vast amounts of money on trimmings. You can simply take lace or ribbon off old clothes – most of the trimmings used in this book once adorned a garment of some kind, before being attacked with a seam ripper! Pearl trimmings, sequins and beads come in rich colours but obviously do not use them if making the doll for a small child.

INTERFACING

Back any small pieces of fabric that fray easily with iron-on interfacing; this is particularly useful for upper body pieces and arms when glittery fabrics are used.

WOOL

Experiment with different colours and textures of wool especially for fantasy characters. Try to collect oddments of wool in sales and use remnants left over from knitting projects. A large ball of wool will usually be enough for two or three dolls.

A trio of characters from around the globe: (from left) Antonio the Ice-Cream Seller (p87); a Downhill Skier (p59) and a Jolly Swagman from 'down under' (p117)

PATTERNS

All patterns are printed full size so that they can be traced straight off the page. Before beginning, check through all the instructions and appropriate pattern pieces.

CUTTING AND TRACING

It is a good idea to have a pencil, ruler, rubber, stiff card, paper and tracing paper handy when making patterns. If you trace patterns onto stiff card, you will be able to use them over and over again. Keep your patterns in labelled envelopes or bags so that they can be found easily.

BODY PATTERNS

The five basic body patterns are given in Chapter 2 together with instructions for making each body.

CLOTHES

Clothes patterns are given for each individual doll, although some patterns will serve several dolls.

SEAMS

5mm (¼in) seams are included on all the appropriate pattern pieces unless otherwise stated.

METHODS

FACES

The positioning of an eye, nose or mouth can determine the character of a doll. All the eyes for the dolls in this book are made from felt; before cutting out the eyes, spread some glue onto one side of the felt and let it dry, then draw the eye on this side and cut it out. Repeat for the other eye and glue both about 2.5cm (1in) apart in the centre of the face and at a slight angle. Spreading the glue onto the back of the felt gives a clean cut edge and prevents it from fraying. Noses can either be drawn on with red pencil or you can make a button nose.

BUTTON NOSE

1 · Cut a piece of stockinette 2cm (1in) square and insert a tiny ball of stuffing in the middle.

2 · Bring the corners of the stockinette together and, with a needle and strong thread, sew a few stitches through the middle, fasten off securely and then trim off the excess fabric (Fig 1).

Fig 1

Mouths are sewn in red thread; see instructions for each Body Pattern in Chapter 2.

All the dolls have glowing rosy cheeks which are simply made by rubbing a blunt red pencil in a circular motion on either side of the face.

HAIRSTYLES

1 · The first hairstyle is very simple; cut eighty pieces of wool each 50cm (20in) in length and tie loosely around the middle with a shorter piece of wool (Fig 2). Glue onto the head and the hair can now either be left long, cut short, fastened in pony tails or tucked under at the back; see individual instructions for each doll.

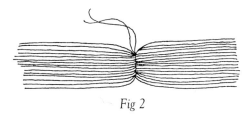

Fig 2

Fig 3

2 · The second hairstyle is for curly hair. Wind several loops of wool around two fingers and make a few stitiches to secure the curls (Fig 3) Continue making curls until you have enough to cover the head, then stitch the curls in place around the head fastening off securely at the top (Fig 4).

Fig 4

MEASUREMENTS

All measurements are given in metric with the imperial equivalent in brackets. Never mix the two measurements since there may be a slight difference which would throw the proportions completely.

Body Patterns

This chapter contains the five basic body patterns you will need to make all the dolls in the book.

Flesh calico, stockinette and toy stuffing are the main materials used to create the bodies, which are quick to make – giving you more time to spend running riot with the clothes and trimmings!

BODY PATTERN 1

MATERIALS

16.5cm (6½in) × 17.5cm (7in) of flesh stockinette
2cm (1in) square of flesh stockinette for the nose
70cm (28in) × 30cm (12in) of flesh calico for the lower body, base and hands
6.5cm (2½in) radius circle of stiff card for the base
Stuffing
Red pencil, black felt and red thread
(See individual instructions for fabric needed for upper body and arms)

BODY

1 · Cut two lower body pieces from calico and two upper body pieces from fabric. With right sides facing, join an upper body to a lower body piece at points A–B (Fig 1).

2 · Press the seams open and, with right sides facing, join around the edge leaving the bottom edges open for turning. Clip any curves and push out to the right side. Turn in the bottom edge 1cm (½in) and tack.

3 · Stuff the body firmly until some of the stuffing actually bulges out from the bottom.

4 · For the base, cut a 6.5cm (2½in) radius circle from stiff card and an 8.5cm (3½in) radius circle from calico. Gather the fabric circle 1cm (½in) from the edge around the card circle, pull up the gathers and fasten off.

5 · Stitch the base around the bottom of the doll (Fig 2).

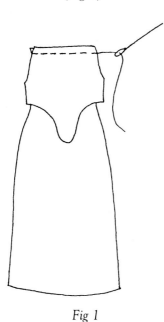

Fig 1

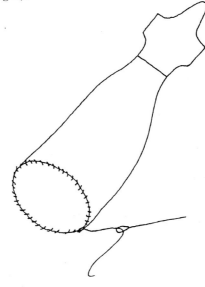

Fig 2

Three lovely ladies! Body Pattern 1 is used for the Christmas Fairy, Body Pattern 3 for the 1920s Flapper and Body Pattern 4 for the Witch

Place on fold

LOWER BODY
Cut 2 in calico

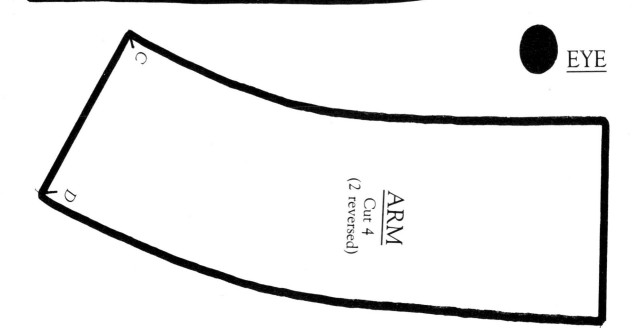

C

D

ARM
Cut 4
(2 reversed)

● EYE

BODY PATTERN 1

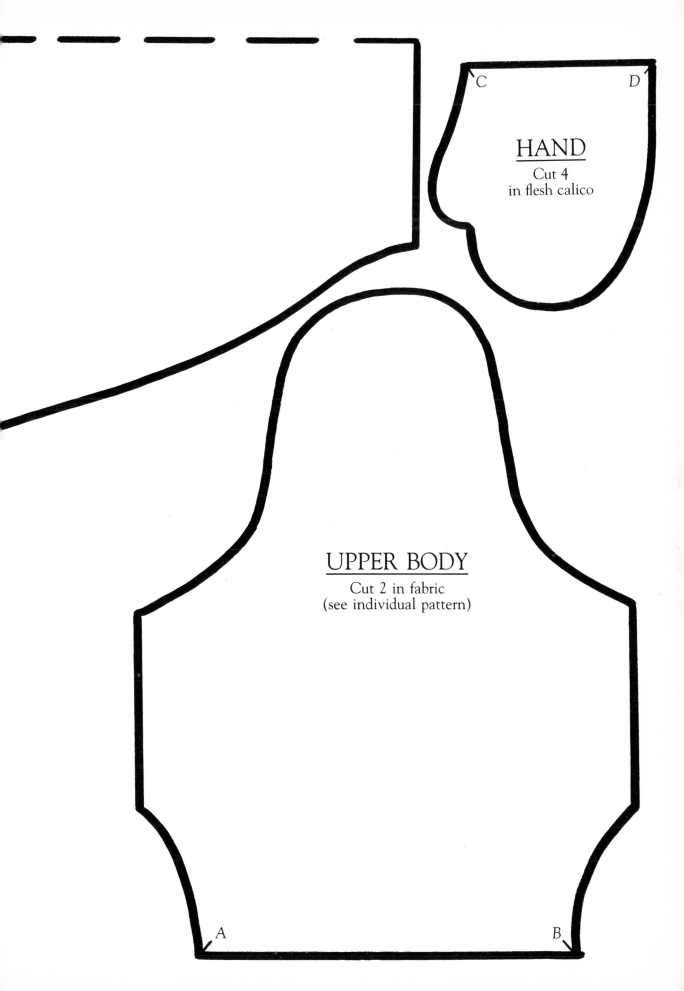

HAND
Cut 4
in flesh calico

C   D

UPPER BODY
Cut 2 in fabric
(see individual pattern)

A   B

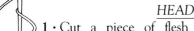

HEAD

1 · Cut a piece of flesh stockinette 16.5cm (6½in) × 17.5cm (7in) with the rib of the fabric running down the width.

2 · Sew the short edges together and then gather the top 1cm (½in) from the edge. Pull up the gathers tightly and fasten off.

3 · Turn out to the right side and stuff into a ball shape to 2cm (1in) from the bottom edge. Gather the bottom 1cm (½in) from the edge and place to one side for a moment.

4 · Spread a little glue onto the pointed top of the body and around the inside edge of the head. Place the head on top of the body, pull up the gathers tightly and fasten off (Fig 3).

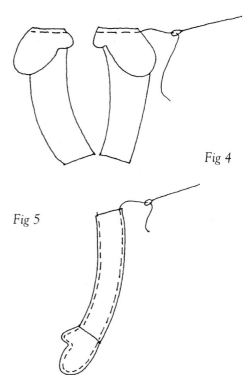

Fig 4

Fig 5

Fig 3

5 · Sew a few stitches through the head into the neck to secure the head firmly.

ARMS

1 · Cut two arms from fabric and two hands from flesh calico. With right sides together, join a hand to each arm matching up points C–D (Fig 4).

2 · Press the seams open and, with right sides together, join both pieces together (Fig 5).

3 · Clip the curves especially around the thumb area and then turn out to the right side.

4 · Gather the top 1cm (½in) from the edge, push in the excess fabric then pull up the gathers tightly and fasten off.

5 · Repeat for the other arm and then glue an arm onto each shoulder pressing down firmly until dry.

FACE

1 · Cut two eyes from black felt and glue halfway down the face 2cm (1in) apart and at a slight angle.

2 · For girl dolls, using black thread, push a long darning needle through the back of the head and sew four stitches 1cm (½in) long on each eye for eyelashes. Push the needle to the back and fasten off.

3 · Make the nose in the same way as described in the Methods section of Chapter 1.

4 · The mouth is simply a 2cm (1in) stitch in red thread under the nose; a small vertical stitch through the middle pulls the mouth into a smile. A small stitch on either side of the mouth gives the doll dimples.

5 · Colour the cheeks as described in the Methods section of Chapter 1.

18

BODY PATTERN 2

MATERIALS

1m (38in) × 50cm (20in) of flesh calico for the body, arms and legs
Black felt, red colouring pencil and red thread
Stuffing

LEGS

1 · Sew the legs together in pairs, right sides facing, down both long edges. Take the sole pieces and stitch to the bottom of each leg (Fig 1).

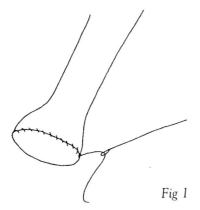

Fig 1

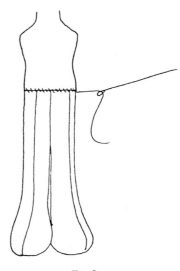

Fig 2

2 · Push out to the right side and stuff each leg to trap the stuffing inside.

BODY

1 · Cut two body pieces from calico and make the neck dart on the wrong side of each piece by folding in half and sewing along the dotted line as shown on the pattern.

2 · With right sides facing, sew the body pieces together down each side leaving the top and bottom edges open. Clip any curves and turn out to the right side.

3 · Turn in the bottom edges of the body 1cm (½in) and trapping the top of each leg inside, tack through all layers and then stitch (Fig 2).

4 · Stuff the body through the top to 2cm (1in) from the top edge. Run a gathering thread 1cm (½in) from the top and, pushing in the excess fabric, pull up the gathers tightly and fasten off (Fig 3).

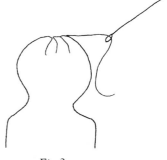

Fig 3

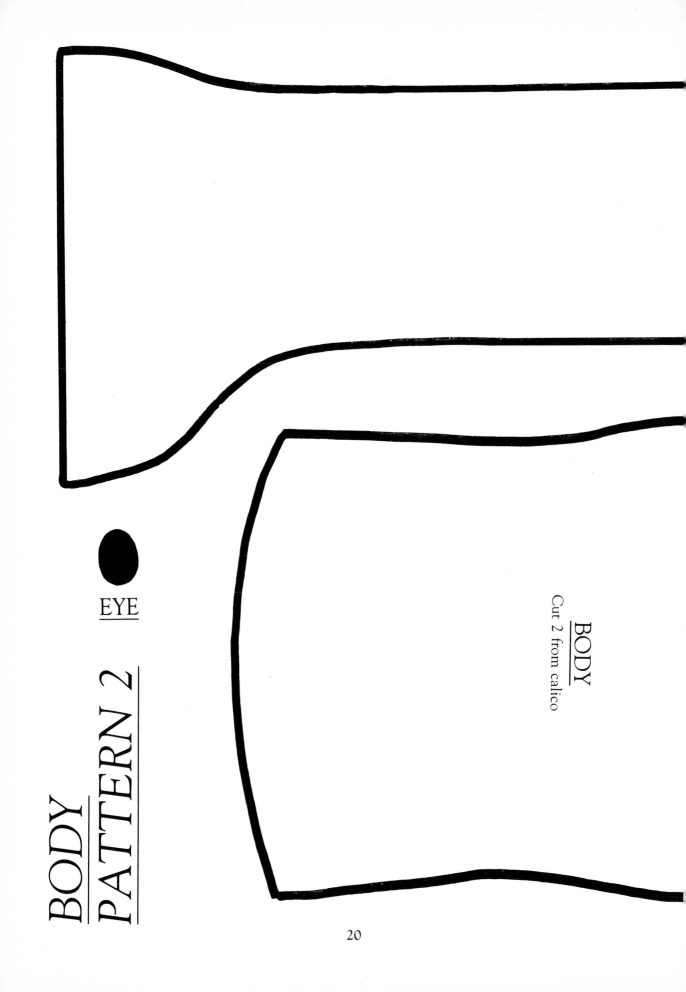

EYE

BODY
PATTERN 2

BODY
Cut 2 from calico

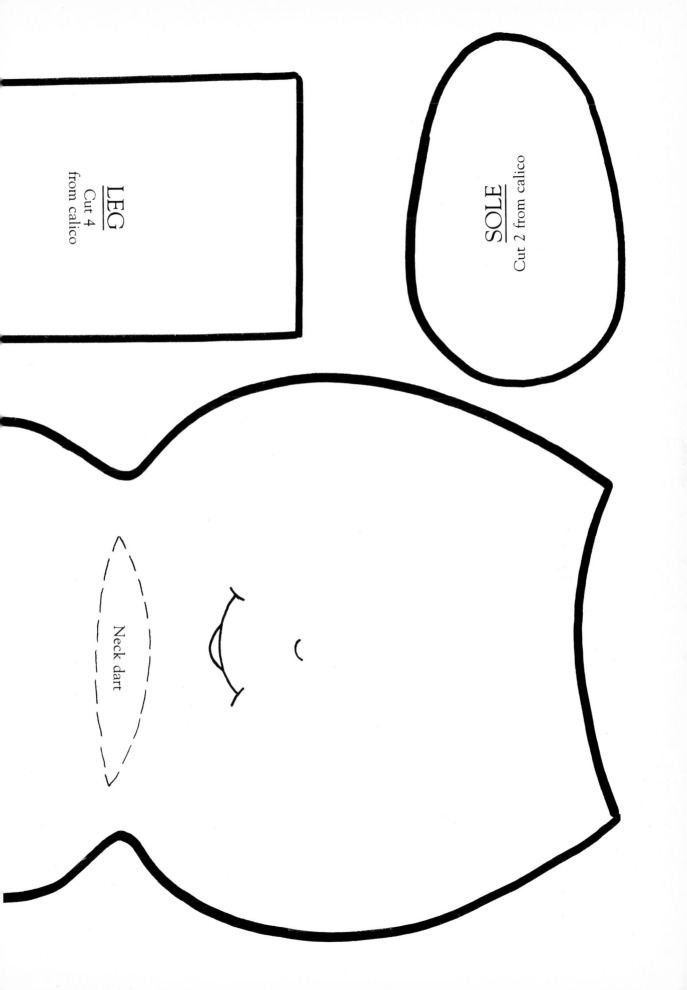

LEG
Cut 4
from calico

SOLE
Cut 2 from calico

Neck dart

ARMS

1 · Join together in pairs, right sides facing, leaving the top straight edge open for turning.

2 · Clip any curves and push out to the right side. Stuff to 1cm (½in) from the top, run a gathering thread 1cm (½in) from the top, push in the excess fabric and pull up the gathers tightly to fasten off.

3 · Glue an arm to each shoulder.

FACE

1 · Cut two eyes from black felt and glue at a slight angle halfway down the face and 2cm (1in) apart. Make the eyelashes for girl dolls as described in Pattern 1.

2 · The nose is simply a curve drawn under the eyes in red pencil as shown on the pattern.

Fig 4

3 · For the mouth, draw lightly onto the face first with pencil following the outline on the pattern. Using stem stitch (Fig 4) sew along both curves. A small stitch on either end of the mouth gives the doll a grin.

ARM
Cut 4
from calico

It's time for a holiday, with Sammy Surfer and a cheerful Downhill Skier (both Body Pattern 2), and an intrepid Diver (Body Pattern 3)

BODY PATTERN 3

MATERIALS

16.5cm (6½in) × 17.5cm (7in) of flesh stockinette for the head
2cm (1in) square of flesh stockinette for the nose
Black felt, red thread and a red pencil
Stuffing
(See individual fabric requirements for body, legs, boots/shoes and arms)

LEGS

1 · Cut four legs and four shoes from fabric using the leg and foot pattern. Taking two shoes and two legs join a shoe to each leg with right sides facing and remembering to reverse one shoe (Fig 1).

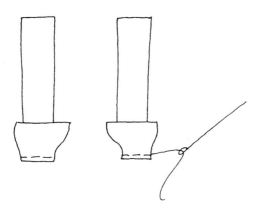

Fig 1

2 · Press the seams open and, with right sides together, join the two pieces leaving the top edge open for turning.

3 · Clip any curves and turn out to the right side. Stuff firmly and tack the top edges together. Repeat for the other leg.

BODY

1 · Using the pattern, cut two from fabric and, with right sides facing, join together around the edge leaving the bottom edge open.
2 · Clip any curves and turn out to the right side. Stuff to 2cm (1in) from the bottom.
3 · Turn in the bottom raw edges 1cm (½in) and trapping the legs in between tack through all layers of fabric then stitch to secure. Remove the tacking stitches.

ARMS

Make the arms in the same way as for Body Pattern 1 following steps 1–5.

HEAD AND FACE

For the head, cut a piece of flesh stockinette 16.5cm (6½in) × 17.5cm (7in) and make in the same way as for Body Pattern 1 following steps 1–5 for the head and steps 1–5 for the face.

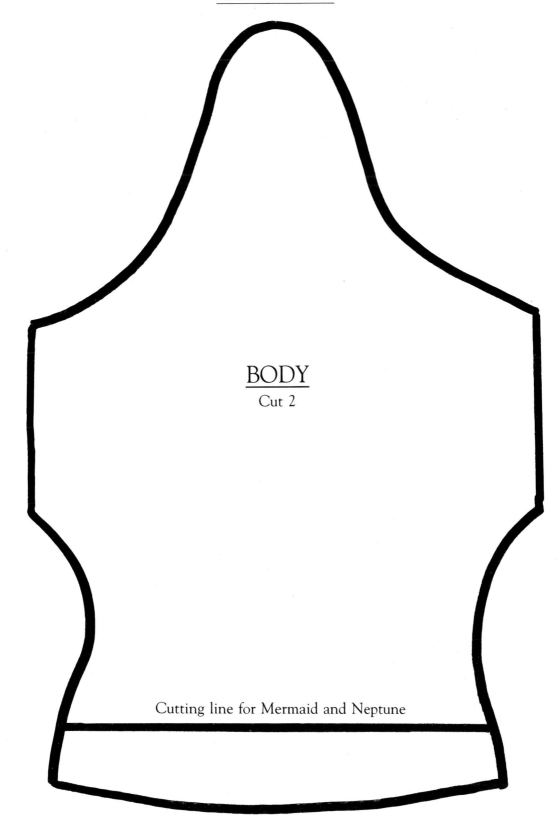

BODY
Cut 2

Cutting line for Mermaid and Neptune

BODY PATTERN 3

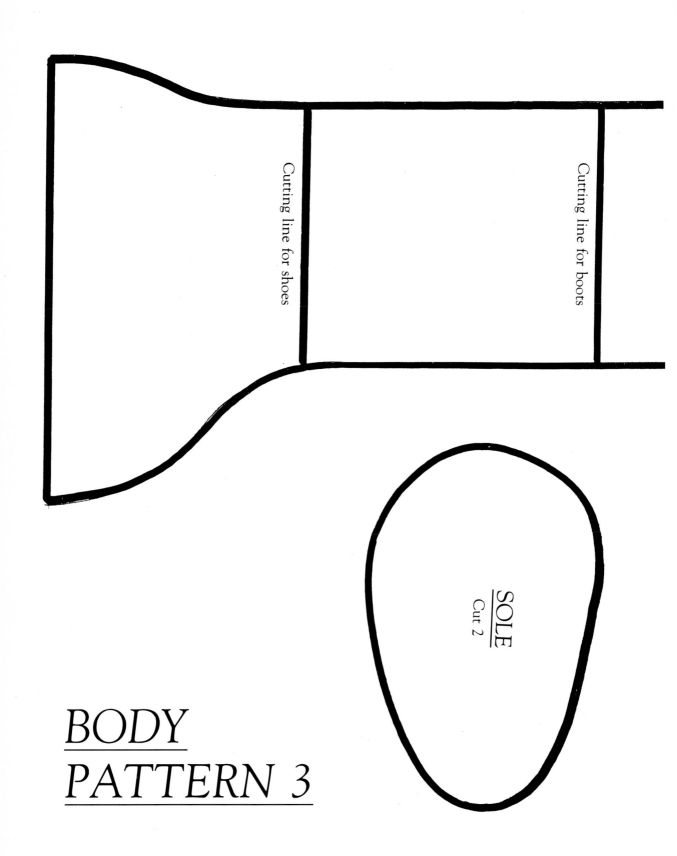

Cutting line for shoes

Cutting line for boots

SOLE
Cut 2

BODY PATTERN 3

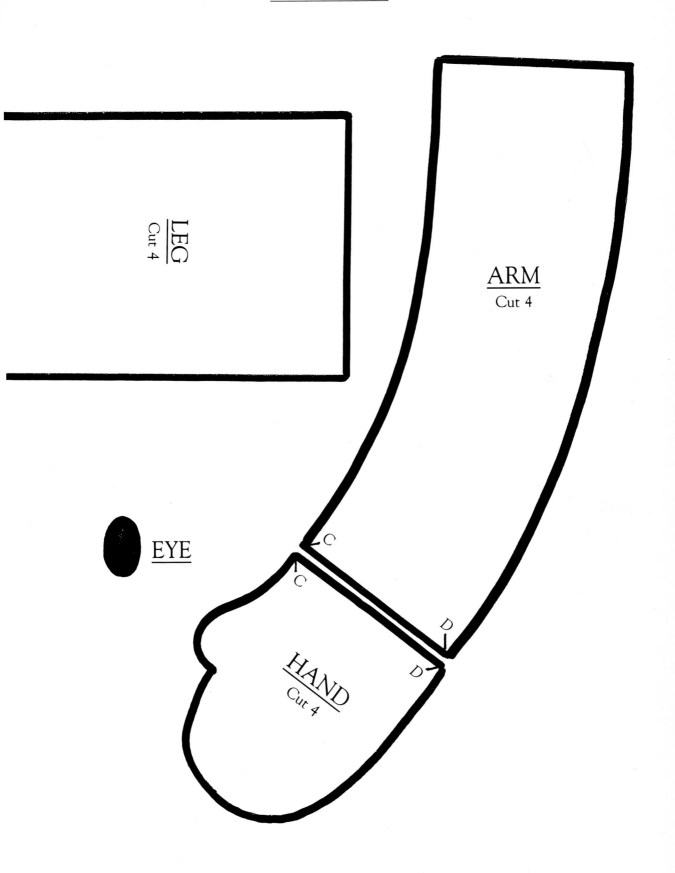

LEG
Cut 4

ARM
Cut 4

EYE

C

C

D

D

HAND
Cut 4

BODY PATTERN 4

MATERIALS

15cm (6in) × 16.5cm (6½in) of flesh stockinette for the head
2cm (1in) square of flesh stockinette for the nose
36cm (14in) × 20cm (8in) of flesh calico for the arms
Black felt, red thread and a red colouring pencil
Stuffing
(See individual fabric requirements for body, legs, and shoes)

BODY

1 · Cut two body pieces from fabric and, with right sides facing, stitch together around the edge from A–B leaving the bottom edge open.
2 · Push out to the right side and stuff to 2cm (1in) from the bottom. Place to one side for a moment.

LEGS

1 · Cut the foot and leg pattern twice in fabric.
2 · Matching up points C–D and, with right sides facing, join a foot to each leg piece (Fig 1).

3 · Fold each leg/foot in half, right sides facing, and stitch the raw edges together (Fig 2).
4 · Clip the curves and turn out to the right side. Suff each leg to 1cm (½in) from the top edge. Tack across the top.
5 · Take the body piece and turn in the bottom edge 1cm (½in). Trap the legs inbetween the bottom edges, tack through all layers and then stitch to secure. Remove the tacking stitches.

ARMS

1 · Cut four arms from calico and sew together, right sides facing, in pairs from points E–F leaving the top straight edge open.
2 · Clip any curves and push out to the right side. Stuff firmly to 1cm (½in) from the top.
3 · Gather the top, push in the excess fabric, pull up the gathers tightly and fasten off.
4 · Glue the arms to each shoulder.

HEAD AND FACE

For the head, cut a piece of flesh stockinette 15 × 16.5cm (6 × 6½in) and make in the same way as for Body Pattern 1 following steps 1–5 for the head and steps 1–5 for the face.

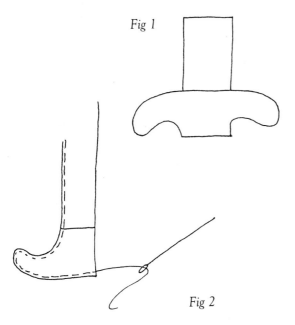

Fig 1

Fig 2

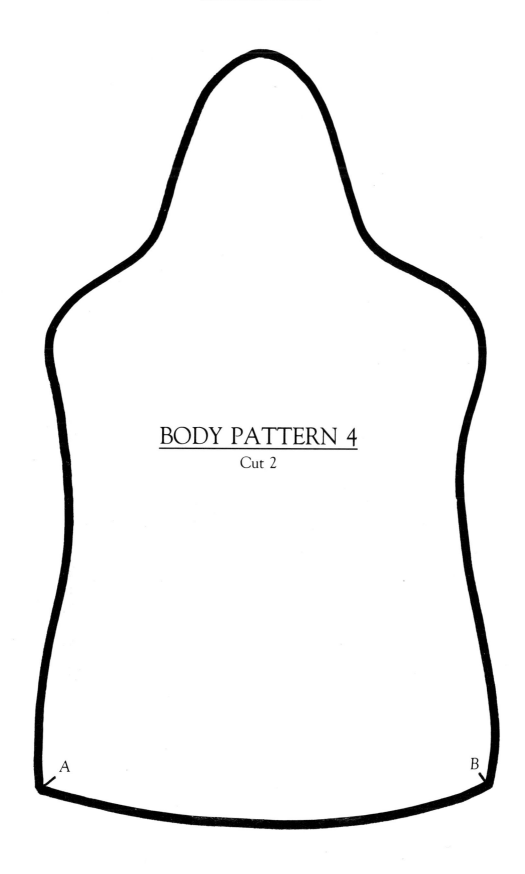

BODY PATTERN 4

Cut 2

A

B

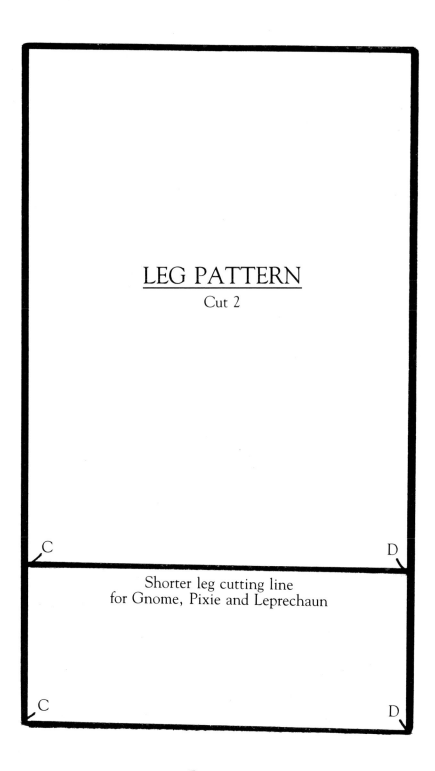

LEG PATTERN

Cut 2

C   D

Shorter leg cutting line
for Gnome, Pixie and Leprechaun

C   D

EYE

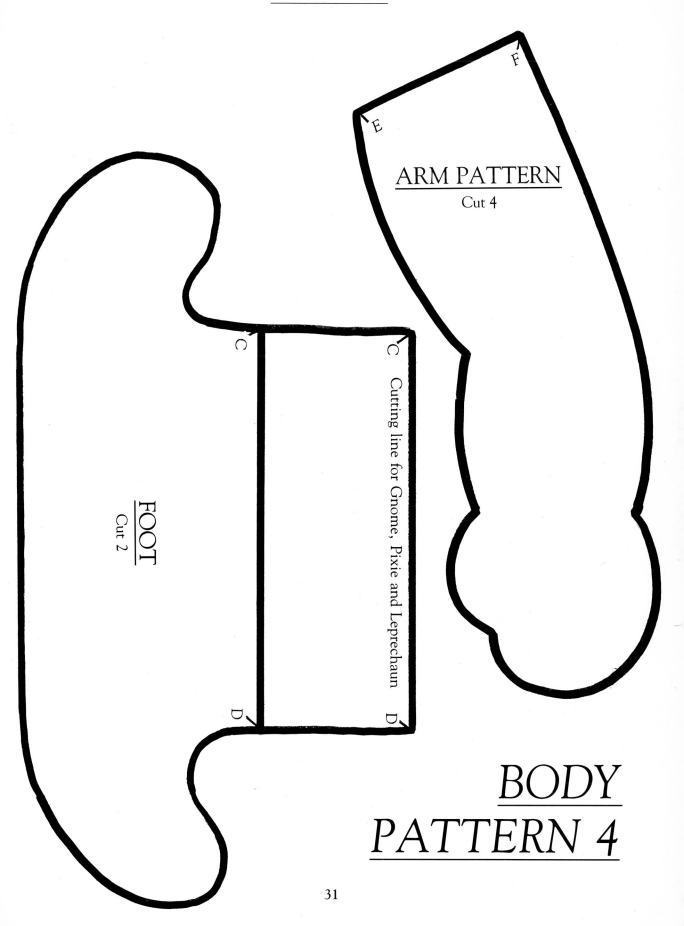

ARM PATTERN
Cut 4

F

E

C C

Cutting line for Gnome, Pixie and Leprechaun

FOOT
Cut 2

D D

BODY
PATTERN 4

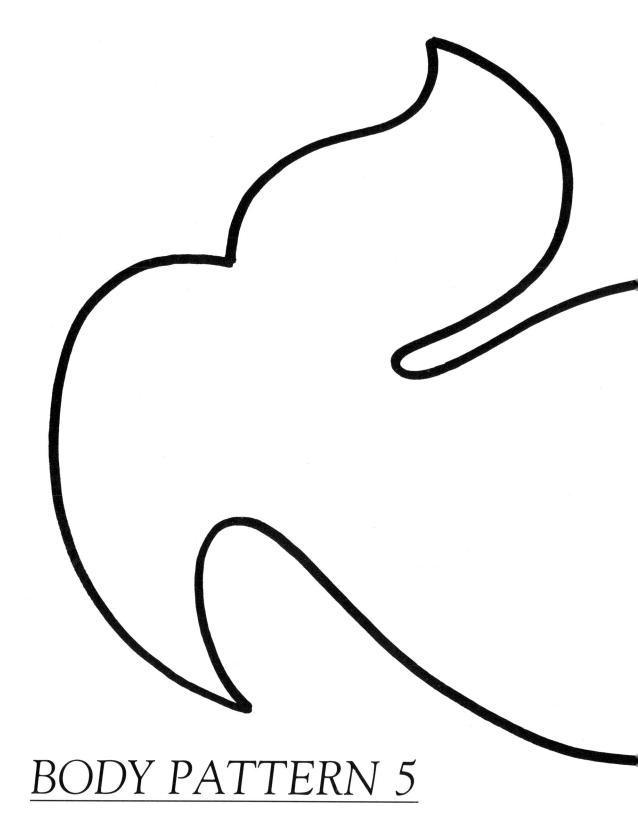

BODY PATTERN 5

BODY PATTERN 5

MATERIALS

16.5cm (6½in) × 17.5cm (7in) of flesh stockinette for the head
(For other materials, see fabric requirements for each mermaid in Chapter 4.)

This fishy tail pattern is for the two mermaids in Chapter 4.
Use the arm pattern from Body Pattern 4 and the body pattern from Body Pattern 3.
Make the head and face as for Body Pattern 1 following steps 1-5 for the head and steps 1-5 for the face.

TAIL PATTERN
Cut 2
in shiny fabric

A

B

Seasonal Dolls

It is always difficult knowing just what to make for a special occasion, but this chapter will provide the answer.

There are ten unusual dolls to make for those important festive times of the year.

So, go on, why not make a Witch for Hallowe'en, a Santa for Christmas or even a King of Hearts on Valentine's Day for your true love?

Five of the best: (from left) Neptune (p75); Titania (p131); Uncle Sam (p52); (seated) a cheeky Pixie (p158) and the Apple Fairy (p148)

QUEEN OF HEARTS

MATERIALS

90cm (36in) × 50cm (19½in) of red taffeta for the upper body, arms and skirt
1m (38in) × 33cm (13in) of heart-patterned fabric for underskirt and sleeves
12cm (4½in) × 10cm (4in) of buckram for the stomacher
12cm (4½in) × 10cm (4in) of silver fabric
15cm (6in) × 6cm (2½in) of shiny red fabric for the motifs
28cm (11in) × 10cm (4in) of buckram for the crown
28cm (11in) × 20cm (8in) of silver fabric
1m (38in) of red sequin trim
50cm (19½in) of glittery red braid
2m (76in) of gathered white lace
30cm (12in) length of red ribbon
36cm (14in) × 5cm (2in) of white fur fabric
Cream wool for hair
2 red ribbon bows

Use Body Pattern 1. For the arms and upper body, use red taffeta.

SKIRT

1 · For the underskirt, cut a piece of heart-patterned fabric, 60cm (24in) x 33cm (13in). Hem the long edge. With right sides facing, join the short edges together and turn out to the right side.

2 · Gather the top 1cm (½in) from the edge to fit around the waist with the seam at the back.

3 · Cut a piece of red taffeta 80cm (32in) × 33cm (13in). Hem the two short edges and one long edge 1cm (½in) and sew white gathered lace to these edges.

4 · Gather the long raw edge to fit around the waist with the opening at the front.

5 · Tie a piece of ribbon around the waist.

STOMACHER

1 · Cut one from buckram and one from silver fabric. Glue the silver fabric onto the buckram and glue glittery braid around the edge.

STOMACHER

CROWN PATTERN
For King & Queen of Hearts

Place on fold

2 · Using the heart pattern, cut two from shiny red fabric and glue on the stomacher as shown on the pattern.

3 · Glue the stomacher onto the front of the doll 5cm (2½in) down from the neck.

SLEEVES

1 · Cut two pieces of heart fabric, each 20cm (8in) × 10cm (4in).

2 · With right sides facing, join the two short edges together on each piece and turn out to the right side.

3 · Turn in the raw edges and gather the top and bottom of both sleeves to fit onto the top of each arm.

4 · Trim the bottom edge of each sleeve with glittery red braid.

CROWN

1 · Using the pattern, cut one from buckram and two from silver fabric.

2 · Glue the silver fabric on either side of the buckram and trim around the pointed edges with red sequin trim.

3 · Cut a strip of white fur fabric 28cm (11in) ×

3.5cm (1½in). Turn in the long edges 1cm (½in) and fold lengthways wrong sides together. Bind the bottom of the crown so that it is sandwiched inbetween the fur.

Pattern for King & Queen of Hearts crown decoration

4 · Using the heart pattern, cut six in shiny red fabric and glue around the crown. Glue the edges together at the back.

HAIR

Make the hair as for Hairstyle 1 in the Methods section of Chapter 1. Tie in a pony tail at the back.

DECORATION

1 · Trim the neck and wrist edges with pleated lace.

2 · Glue a red bow on each corner of the skirt.

KING OF HEARTS

MATERIALS

90cm (36in) × 50cm (19½in) of red taffeta for skirt, body and arms
25cm (9½in) of shiny fabric to trim the waist
28cm (11in) × 10cm (4in) of buckram for the crown
28cm (11in) × 20cm (8in) of silver fabric
1m (38in) of red sequin trim
36cm (14in) × 5cm (2in) of white fur fabric for the crown
30cm (12in) square of shiny red fabric for heart motifs
80cm (32in) x 43cm (17in) of silver fabric for the cape
160cm (64in) of glittery red braid
Cream wool for the hair and beard

Use Body Pattern 1. Make the upper body and arms in red taffeta.

SKIRT
Make the skirt in the same way as for the Queen of Hearts underskirt, following steps 1 and 2.

CAPE
1 · Cut a piece of silver fabric 80cm (32in) × 40cm (16in).

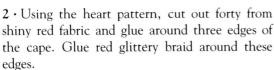

Pattern for King of Hearts decoration

2 · Using the heart pattern, cut out forty from shiny red fabric and glue around three edges of the cape. Glue red glittery braid around these edges.
3 · Gather the remaining long edge to fit around the neck and fasten off securely.

HAIR
Make the hair as for Hairstyle 1 in the Methods section of Chapter 1, leave it loose and trim it to shoulder length (Fig 1).

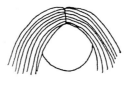
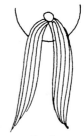

Fig 1

Fig 2

BEARD
1 · Cut forty pieces of cream wool each 30cm (12in) long, tie around the middle with a short length of wool.
2 · Glue onto the face just under the nose letting the beard flop down (Fig 2).

CROWN
Make in exactly the same way as for the Queen of Hearts and glue onto the head.

TRIMMINGS
Glue glittery red braid around each wrist for added decoration.

EASTER PARADE DOLL

MATERIALS

1m (38in) square of lemon satin for underskirt, arms and body
1m (38in) square of lemon organza for the puff sleeves, overskirt and hat
30cm (12in) × 23cm (9in) of buckram for the hat
Small artificial flowers for the hat
2m (76in) of pleated lace to trim the bottom of the skirt and wrists
1m (38in) of 5cm (2in) wide lemon ribbon
1m (38in) of lemon braid
Brown wool for hair

Use Body Pattern 1. For the upper body and arms use lemon satin.

SKIRT

1 · Cut one piece each of lemon satin and lemon organza 60cm (24in) × 33cm (13in).
2 · Hem one long edge on both pieces and sew three layers of pleated lace to the hemmed edge of the organza piece.
3 · With right sides together, join the short edges of both pieces and turn out to the right side.
4 · Fit the organza skirt over the satin one and gathering through both layers 1cm (½in) from the edge fit around the waist. Pull up the gathers tightly and fasten off.
5 · Trim the waist edge with ribbon and braid.

SLEEVES

Make in the same way as the Queen of Hearts following steps 1–4. Instead of red braid, trim with lemon braid.

HAIR

Make as for Hairstyle 1 as described in the Methods section of Chapter 1 using brown wool. Tie in a pony tail at the back.

HAT

1 · Using brim pattern, cut one from buckram.

2 · Cut a strip of lemon organza 90cm (36in) × 14cm (5½in) and fold in half lengthways. Pleat around the edge of the hat with the buckram sandwiched inbetween the fold (Fig 1).

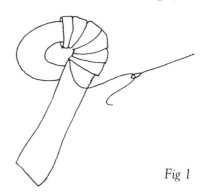

Fig 1

3 · Turn in the raw edges and overlap the ends.
4 · Cut the crown from organza and with right sides facing and raw edges together, sew around the inner edge of the brim pleating the fabric slightly as you sew (Fig 2).
5 · Trim around the edge of the brim with artificial flowers and glue the hat onto the head at a slight angle.

Fig 2

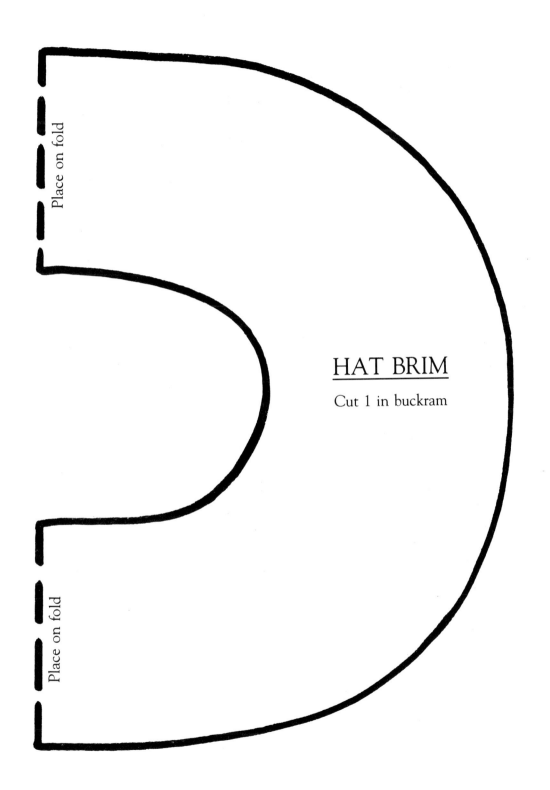

Place on fold

Place on fold

HAT BRIM

Cut 1 in buckram

TRIMMINGS

1 · The neck bow is made by cutting a piece of 5cm (2in) wide lemon ribbon 23cm (9in) long. Fold the ends over to meet at the back.

2 · Gather through the middle and fasten off securely (Fig 3). Cover the middle with a folded strip of ribbon.

3 · Make the strands from two 10cm (4in) pieces of ribbon by cutting the ends into points. Sew onto the back of the bow to finish (Fig 4).

4 · Glue the bow just under the chin.

5 · Trim the wrists with pleated lace and braid if desired.

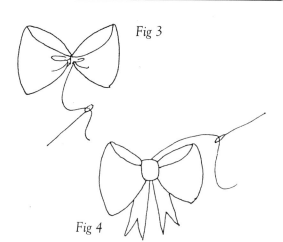

Fig 3

Fig 4

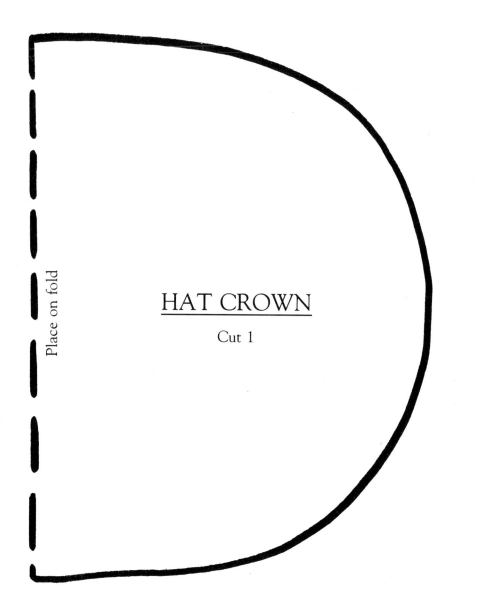

Place on fold

HAT CROWN

Cut 1

JUNE BRIDE

MATERIALS

90cm (36in) × 50cm (19½in) of white satin for underskirt, upper body and arms
22cm (8½in) × 12cm (5in) of white satin for the puff sleeves
1m (38in) × 80cm (32in) of non-fray white spotted organza for skirt and neck frill
20cm (8in) length of 5cm (2in) wide pink satin ribbon to trim the waist
Pearl trimming and diamante for the necklace
Pink fabric flowers for headdress and posy
Pink ribbon, pearl trimming and lace to trim posy
1m (38in) × 56cm (22in) of white netting for the veil
Small mother-of-pearl sequins to decorate the veil
Brown wool for hair

Use Body Pattern 1. Use white satin for the upper body and arms.

SKIRT

1 · Cut a piece of white satin 80cm (32in) × 33cm (13in), hem one long edge and, with right sides facing, sew the two side edges together.
2 · Turn out to the right side and gather the top raw edge around the waist.
3 · From spotted organza, cut a piece 80cm (32in) × 33cm (13in), a piece 80cm (32in) × 24cm (9½in) and a piece 80cm (32in) × 16cm (6½in). Scallop one long edge on all three pieces as for the Christmas Fairy (p66).
4 · Place all the pieces on top of each other with the smallest one on top and gather through all the layers along the remaining long raw edge around the waist. Fasten off securely.
5 · Trim the waist edge with the wide pink satin ribbon.

SLEEVES

Make the sleeves as for the Queen of Hearts, but use white satin and omit the red braid.

NECK FRILL

1 · Cut a piece of spotted organza 80cm (32in) × 6cm (2½in) and gather along one long edge to fit around the shoulders.
2 · Secure with a few stitches.

HAIR

Using brown wool, make as for Hairstyle 1 as described in the Methods section of Chapter 1. Leave the hair long.

HEADDRESS AND VEIL

1 · Sew several artificial flowers onto the front of the head for the headdress.
2 · Cut a 1m (38in) × 56cm (22in) piece of netting for the veil. Glue a mother-of-pearl sequin here and there for added glitter.
3 · Gather one long edge to measure about 6cm (2½in) and glue just behind the headdress.

POSY

1 · Sew two lengths of ribbon and a length of pearl beading to a bunch of artificial flowers.
2 · Sew some lace behind the flowers and then sew the posy onto one of the hands.

TRIMMINGS

Decorate the neck edge with pearl trimming and diamante for a necklace.

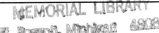

WITCH

MATERIALS

30cm (12in) × 23cm (9in) of black glittery fabric for the body
25cm (10in) × 21cm (8in) of red/white striped fabric for the legs
30cm (12in) square of black felt for the hat
20cm (8in) square of buckram for the hat brim
15cm (6in) × 10cm (4in) of silver fabric for the bow
50cm (19½in) of silver ric-rac braid
30cm (12in) × 21cm (8in) of blue shiny fabric for the shoes and waistband
70cm (27½in) × 25cm (10in) of black taffeta for the cape
1.5m (57in) of silver braid
80cm (32in) × 60cm (24in) of non-fray purple organza for the skirt
80cm (32in) × 40cm (16in) of non-fray green organza for the skirt
50cm (19½in) of blue sequin trim
Small piece of black braid to trim ankles
Small silver star sequins
Length of green ribbon to tie the cape
Purple wool for the hair

Use Body Pattern 4. Use glittery black fabric for the bodice, red striped fabric for the legs and shiny blue fabric for the shoes.

SKIRT

1 · From purple organza cut a piece 60cm (23½in) × 20cm (8½in), a piece 60cm (23½in) × 17cm (6½in) and a piece 60cm (23½in) × 11cm (4½in). Cut zig-zags along one long edge on each piece (Fig 1).
2 · From green organza cut a piece 60cm (23½in) × 10cm (4in) and a piece 60cm (23½in) × 20cm (8in). Zig-zag the long edges as for the purple organza.

3 · Place the long straight edges of all the skirt pieces together alternating the colours. Gather through all the layers and sew around the waist.
4 · Glue on silver star sequins.
5 · Trim the waist with a 3cm (1in) × 25cm (10in) piece of shiny blue fabric. Overlap the back edges and sew in place. Trim with blue sequins.

CAPE

1 · Cut a piece of black taffeta 70cm (27½in) × 25cm (10in). Hem three edges and glue silver braid to these edges.
2 · Gather the remaining long edge around the neck.
3 · Tie a length of green ribbon in a bow and glue at the neck edge.

HAIR

Use purple wool and make as described for Hairstyle 1 in the Methods section of Chapter 1.
· Leave the hair long.

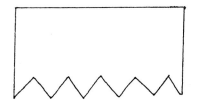

Fig 1

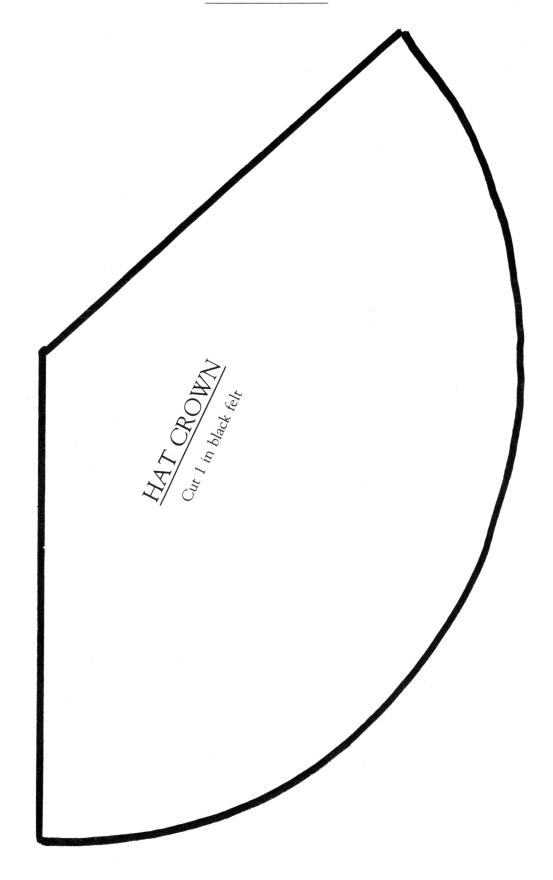

HAT CROWN
Cut 1 in black felt

HAT

1 · Cut a brim once in buckram and twice in black felt. Glue the felt onto either side of the buckram.

2 · Cut the crown from black felt and sew the two short edges together. Push out to the right side.

3 · With right sides together, slipstitch the bottom edge of the brim to the inner edge of the crown (Fig 2).

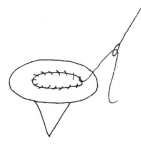

Fig 2

4 · Decorate the brim with silver ric-rac braid. The bow is simply made from a piece of silver fabric 15cm (6in) × 10cm (4in). With right sides facing, join the short edges and turn out to the right side. Gather through the middle, cover with a folded strip of fabric and glue onto the front of the hat.

Fig 3

DECORATIONS

Glue star sequins onto the hat and glue black braid around each ankle for added decoration (Fig 3).

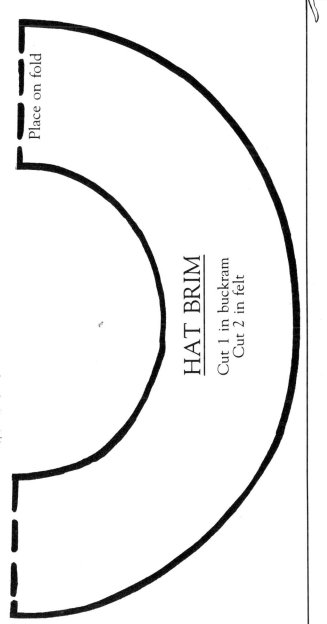

Place on fold

HAT BRIM

Cut 1 in buckram
Cut 2 in felt

WIZARD

MATERIALS

90cm (36in) x 50cm (19½in) of gold/blue striped fabric for skirt, upper body and arm
56cm (22in) of black velvet ribbon
80cm (32in) × 43cm (17in) of glittery blue fabric for the cape
30cm (12in) × 15cm (6in) of buckram for the collar
30cm (12in) square of glittery blue fabric
1m (38in) of silver braid to trim the collar
2m (76in) of silver ric-rac braid to trim the cape
40cm (16in) × 20cm (8in) of buckram for the hat
40cm (16in) × 20cm (8in) of purple felt
36cm (14in) of silver/white braid to trim around hat
2m (76in) of glittery purple braid for the hat and skirt
30cm (12in) garden stick and gold ribbon for the wand
Grey wool for the hair and beard

Use Body Pattern 1. For the arms and upper body use gold/blue striped fabric.

SKIRT

1 · Cut a piece of gold/blue striped fabric 60cm (24in) × 33cm (13in). Hem one long edge and glue two tiers of glittery purple braid to it.
2 · With right sides facing, join the short edges, turn out to the right side, place on the doll and then gather to fit around the waist 1cm (½in) from the edge.
3 · Cut two pieces of black velvet ribbon, each 28cm (11in) long. Wrap one around the waist, overlapping at the back and stitching the ends down. Place the other piece slightly above the first around the waist, overlapping the edges slightly and stitching down at the back in the same way.

CAPE

1 · Cut a piece of glittery blue fabric 80cm (32in) × 40cm (16in). Hem three edges and glue silver ric-rac braid to these edges.
2 · Gather the long raw edge to fit the neck.
3 · Using the collar pattern, cut one from buckram and two from glittery blue fabric. Glue

the glittery fabric onto either side of the buckram.
4 · Trim around the outer curved edge and short edges with silver ric-rac braid. Sew or glue the inner curved edge onto the back of the neck.

HAIR AND BEARD

Using grey wool, make as for The King of Hearts, but for the beard, use strips of wool 50cm (19½in) long.

HAT

1 · Using the pattern, cut one from buckram and one from purple felt. Glue the felt onto one side of the buckram.
2 · Spread glue onto one back edge and overlap both edges pressing down firmly until dry. You should now have the basic cone shape.
3 · Sew six 16cm (6½in) strips of glittery purple braid down the length of the hat and trim the bottom edge with silver braid. Glue securely onto the head.

WAND

Using a 30cm (12in) garden stick, wrap gold ribbon around and sew to one of the hands.

COLLAR

Cut 1 in buckram
Cut 2 in fabric

Place to fold

Place on fold

HAT

Cut 1 from buckram
Cut 1 from felt

UNCLE SAM

MATERIALS

48cm (19in) × 42cm (16½in) of cream satin for the body and arms
32cm (12½in) × 20cm (8in) of flesh calico for the legs
51cm (20in) × 15cm (6in) of black felt for the shoes
56cm (22in) × 30cm (12in) or red/white striped fabric for the trousers
30cm (12in) length of 1cm (½in) elastic
30cm (12in) × 21cm (8½in) of blue felt for the waistcoat
20cm (8in) × 10cm (4in) of red/white striped fabric for the waistcoat
Small silver star sequins, silver ric-rac braid and glittery blue braid
20cm (8in) square of buckram for the hat brim
42cm (16½in) × 35cm (13½in) of blue felt for the hat brim, crown and side
17cm (6½in) × 11cm (4in) of red/white striped fabric for the side of the hat
1.5m (57in) of red sequin trim and large silver star sequins to trim the hat
20cm (8in) × 12cm (4½in) of blue satin for the bow tie
Small piece of white felt for the beard and moustache
White wool for hair

Use Body Pattern 3. Use black felt for the shoes, flesh calico for the legs and cream satin for the body and arms.

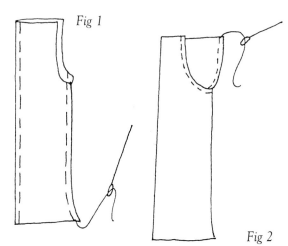

Fig 1

Fig 2

TROUSERS

1 · Cut two front pieces and two back pieces from red/white striped fabric remembering to reverse two pieces.

2 · With right sides facing, join one back piece and one front piece together down each side (Fig 1).

3 · Turn one leg right side out and fit inside the other leg with right sides facing.

4 · Sew together along the curved inside leg edges. Clip the curves and turn out to the right side (Fig 2).

5 · Hem the bottom of each leg 1cm (½in) and hem the waist edge 2cm (1in) leaving a gap to thread elastic through.

6 · Thread elastic through the casing, fit the trousers onto the doll and pull up the elastic tightly around the waist edge.

WAISTCOAT

1 · Cut a back piece and a front piece from blue felt. Cut the other front piece in red/white striped fabric remembering to reverse the pattern.

2 · With right sides facing, join the front pieces to the back piece at the shoulder seams. Turn out to the right side.

WAISTCOAT BACK

Cut 1

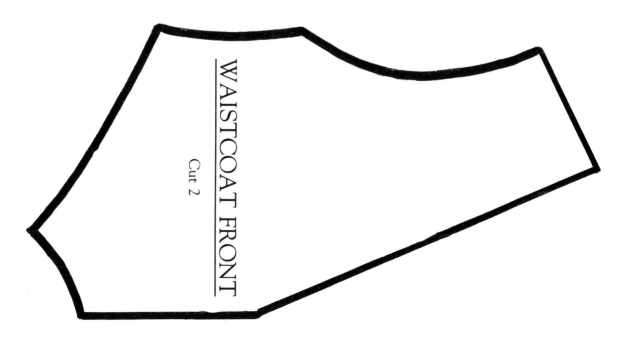

WAISTCOAT FRONT

Cut 2

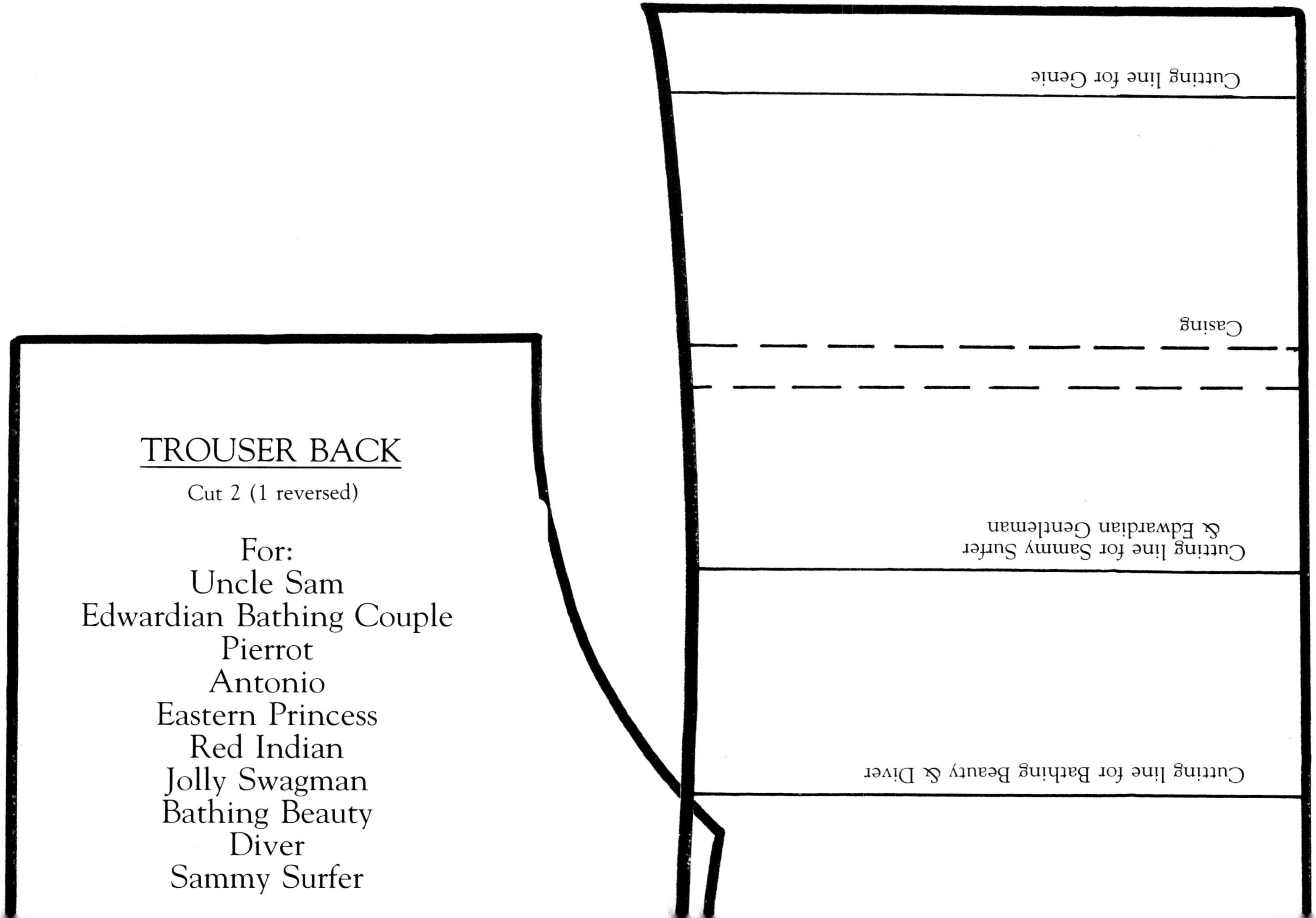

Cutting line for Genie

Casing

Cutting line for Sammy Surfer
& Edwardian Gentleman

Cutting line for Bathing Beauty & Diver

TROUSER BACK

Cut 2 (1 reversed)

For:
Uncle Sam
Edwardian Bathing Couple
Pierrot
Antonio
Eastern Princess
Red Indian
Jolly Swagman
Bathing Beauty
Diver
Sammy Surfer

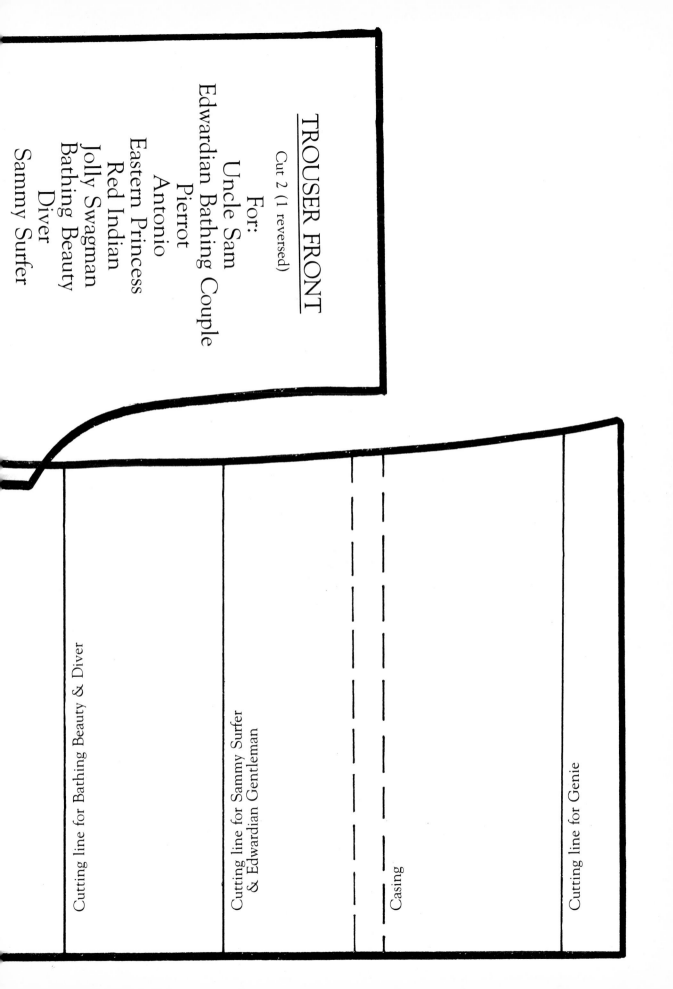

TROUSER FRONT

Cut 2 (1 reversed)

For:
Uncle Sam
Edwardian Bathing Couple
Pierrot
Antonio
Eastern Princess
Red Indian
Jolly Swagman
Bathing Beauty
Diver
Sammy Surfer

Cutting line for Bathing Beauty & Diver

Cutting line for Sammy Surfer & Edwardian Gentleman

Casing

Cutting line for Genie

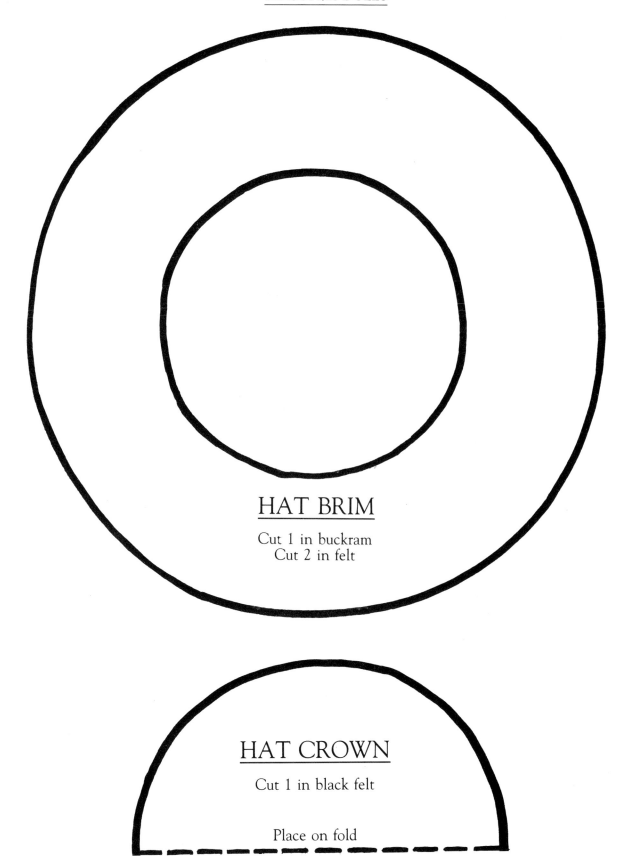

HAT BRIM

Cut 1 in buckram
Cut 2 in felt

HAT CROWN

Cut 1 in black felt

Place on fold

3 · Trim around the edge with silver ric-rac braid and around the armholes with glittery blue braid.

4 · Fit the waistcoat onto the doll; you may need to bend the arms slightly. Sew silver star sequins onto the blue side of the waistcoat.

HAT

1 · Cut the brim as for the Witch once in buckram and twice in blue felt. Glue the felt onto both sides of the buckram piece.

2 · For the sides, cut a piece of blue felt and a piece of red/white striped fabric each 9cm (3½in) × 11cm (4½in).

3 · With right sides together, join the short edges. Cut the crown from blue felt and slipstitch around the top of the sides (Fig 3).

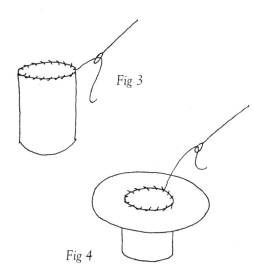

Fig 3

Fig 4

4 · Push out to the right side and stitch the lower raw edge to the inner edge of the brim (Fig 4).

5 · Sew red sequin trim around the hat brim and crown. Sew large star sequins onto the blue section of the side.

BOW TIE

1 · Cut a piece of blue satin 16cm (6½in) × 10cm (4in). Fold the long edges over to meet at the back.

2 · Fold the side edges over to meet at the back and then gather through the middle, pull up the gathers tightly and fasten off. Trim around the middle with a small strip of fabric.

3 · Glue on the doll just under the chin.

HAIR

Make as for the Wizard but use white wool.

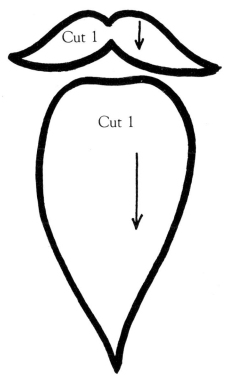

Cut 1

Cut 1

Beard & Moustache Pattern

BEARD AND MOUSTACHE

1 · Using the pattern, cut a moustache and beard from white felt.

2 · Glue the beard just under the nose and the moustache on top.

DECORATION

Trim the wrist edges with blue braid.

DOWNHILL SKIER

MATERIALS

50cm (19½in) × 40cm (16in) of quilted fabric for the salopettes
1m (38in) × 20cm (8in) of white fleece fabric or felt for the jumper
1.5m (57in) of blue bias binding
Small length of velcro
40cm (16in) × 20cm (8in) of white fur fabric
Small piece of white ribbon for shoes
60cm (24in) × 20cm (8in) of pink felt for shoes and logo
Two 30cm (12in) garden sticks and green ribbon for ski poles
40cm (16in) × 15cm (6in) of stiff card for skis
40cm (16in) × 15cm (6in) of green felt
25cm (10in) × 15cm (6in) of gold fabric to trim skis
Ginger coloured wool for hair

Use Body Pattern 2.

This doll has a slightly different eye pattern to the others.

1 · Using the pattern, cut two eye backing pieces from white felt and two pupils from blue felt.

Eye Pattern

2 · Glue the pupils onto the backing pieces and glue the eyes onto the face about 3cm (1½in) apart and at a slight angle.

SALOPETTES

Before you begin join the pattern pieces together as indicated on the pattern.

1 · Using the pattern, cut two (one reversed) from quilted fabric.

2 · With right sides facing, sew together along both the centre front and centre back curved edges.

3 · Open out and sew the inside leg (Fig 1).

4 · Push out to the right side and trim the bottom of each leg with fur fabric. Trim around the top edge with bias binding.

5 · Cut two strips of quilted fabric each 22cm (8½in) × 2.5cm (1in). Fold the long edges over to the back and slipstitch together. Fold over the ends of each piece 1cm (½in) and stitch down.

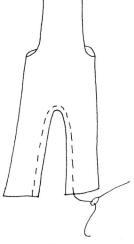

Fig 1

6 · Cross the straps over at the back and stitch down (Fig 2).

7 · Sew velcro onto the ends of each strip and also a piece on either side of the front 3.5cm (1½in) down from the top. Place the salopettes to one side.

Fig 2

JUMPER

1 · Cut out bodice and sleeves in white fleece or felt and, with right sides together, join a back piece to each shoulder.

2 · Open out and join a sleeve to each armhole gathering slightly (Fig 3).

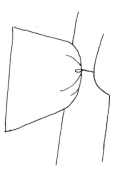

Fig 3

3 · Fold the sleeve and sew across the arm and down the side of the bodice. Repeat for the other side.

4 · Push out to the right side and hem the back edges 1.5cm (½in).

5 · Trim the neck edge with bias binding and then fit the bodice onto the doll, overlapping the back edges and stitching down.

Now fit the salopettes onto the doll bringing the straps over to the front.

SHOES

1 · Join the back seams of the shoes and, with the right sides together, sew the sole to the bottom of the shoe, matching up the centre points.

2 · Sew a length of ribbon to each side of the shoe. Repeat for the other shoe and fit onto the doll.

HEADBAND

1 · Cut a piece of white fur fabric 40cm (16in) × 8cm (4in). Fold over the long edges to meet at the back, turn in the ends and stitch down.

2 · Sew velcro to one end and to the inside edge of the other end. Place around the head.

SKIS

1 · Cut two pieces of stiff card, each 40cm (16in) × 6cm (2½in) and round off the ends of both pieces. Glue green felt on both sides of each piece.

2 · Using the pattern, cut four zig-zag pieces from gold fabric remembering to reverse two pieces and glue onto each ski.

3 · Glue one half of a piece of velcro to each ski and the other half onto the bottom of each shoe. The skis can now be attached to the shoes for a realistic effect.

SKI POLES

Simply cover two 30cm (12in) garden sticks with green ribbon. Tie a loop of ribbon to each stick so that they can be held in each hand.

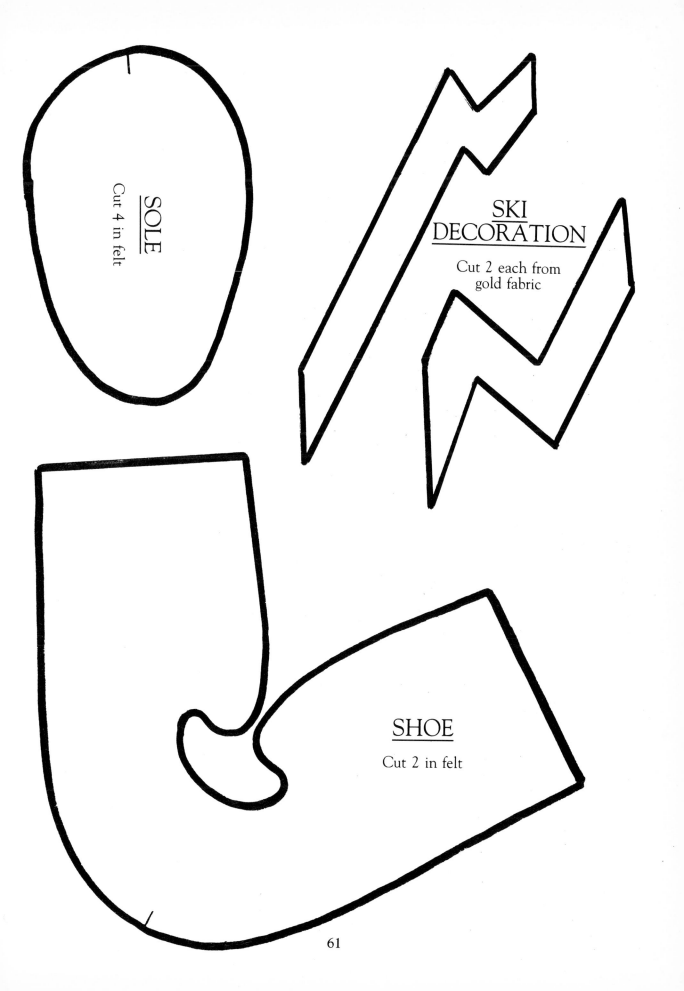

SOLE

Cut 4 in felt

SKI
DECORATION

Cut 2 each from
gold fabric

SHOE

Cut 2 in felt

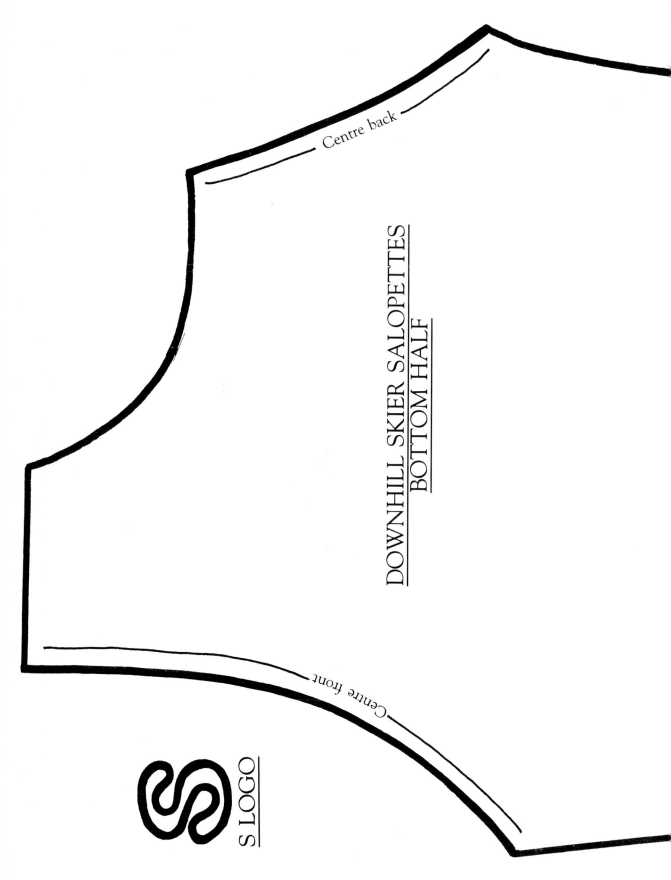

Centre back

DOWNHILL SKIER SALOPETTES
BOTTOM HALF

Centre front

S LOGO

Join pattern along this line

Join pattern along this line

SALOPETTES
TOP HALF

Cut 2 in quilted fabric
(1 reversed)

B

B

A

A

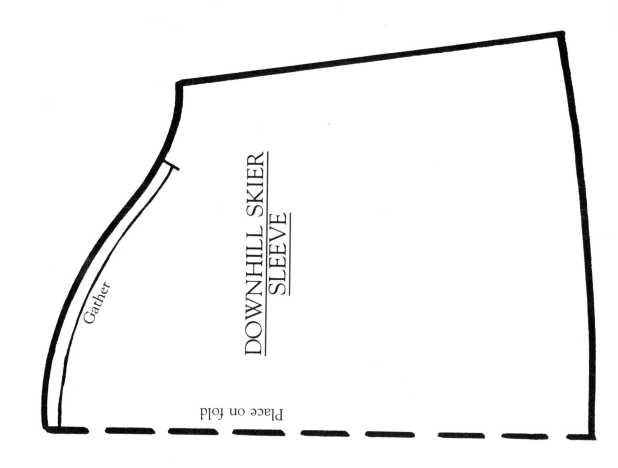

DOWNHILL SKIER
SLEEVE

Gather

Place on fold

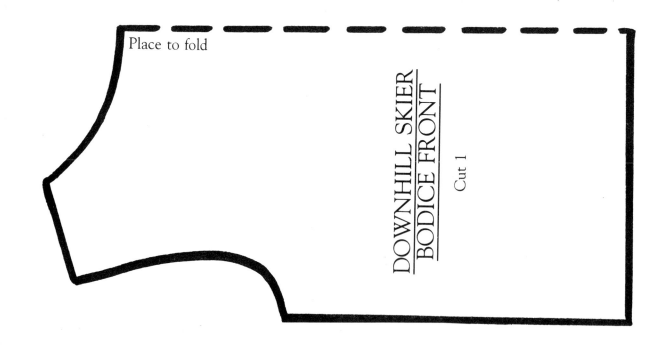

Place to fold

DOWNHILL SKIER
BODICE FRONT

Cut 1

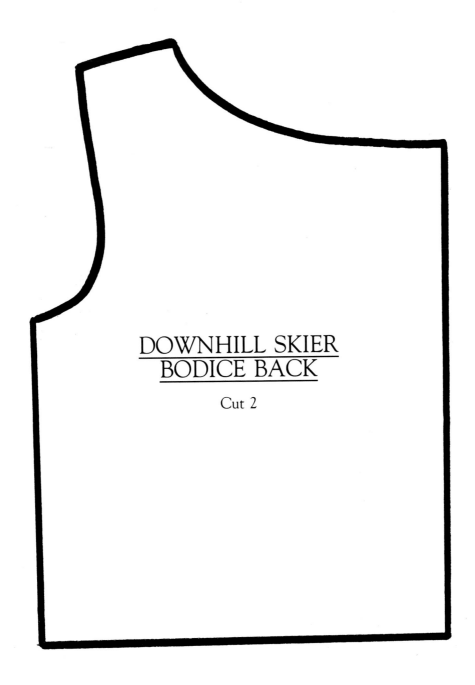

DOWNHILL SKIER
BODICE BACK

Cut 2

CHRISTMAS FAIRY

MATERIALS

90cm (36in) × 50cm (19½in) of gold fabric for the skirt, upper body and arms
80cm (32in) × 50cm (19½in) of gold net
40cm (16in) × 30cm (12in) of shiny fabric for the wings and belt
40cm (16in) x 30cm (12in) of buckram
2m (76in) of gold glittery braid (or use a selection of braids, as in the photograph)
2m (76in) of gold net
28cm (11in) × 10cm (4in) of buckram for the crown
28cm (11in) × 20cm (8in) of gold fabric
20cm (8in) pipecleaner
Glittery pink braid, a shiny button and a small piece of gold net to trim the wand
Pearl beading and sequins or diamante to decorate the dress
Pink wool for the hair

Use Body Pattern 1. For the arms and upper body use gold fabric.

SKIRT

1 · Cut a piece of gold fabric 80cm (32in) × 33cm (13in) and sew gold braid to one long edge. With right sides facing, sew the short edges together and turn out to the right side.
2 · Gather the top 1cm (½in) from the edge, place on the doll and pull up the gathers tightly around the waist fastening off securely.
3 · Cut a piece of gold net 80cm (32in) × 24cm (9½in) and a piece 80cm (32in) × 16cm (6½in). Scallop a long edge on both pieces (Fig 1).

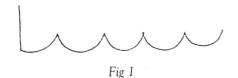

Fig 1

4 · Place the small piece on top of the larger piece with raw edges together and gather to fit around the waist over the gold underskirt.

BELT

1 · Using the pattern, cut one from buckram and one slightly bigger all round from shiny fabric.
2 · Glue the buckram to the wrong side of the shiny fabric. Snip the edges of the shiny fabric to make little flaps, then glue the flaps over to the wrong side of the belt (Fig 2).

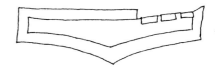

Fig 2

3 · Glue the belt around the waist, overlapping the ends at the back and sewing together.

WINGS

1 · Using the pattern, cut one from buckram and one from shiny fabric. Place the shiny piece on top of the buckram, tack around the edge and then stitch. Remove the tacking stitches.
2 · Using a long darning needle and strong thread, sew the wings to the back of the doll.

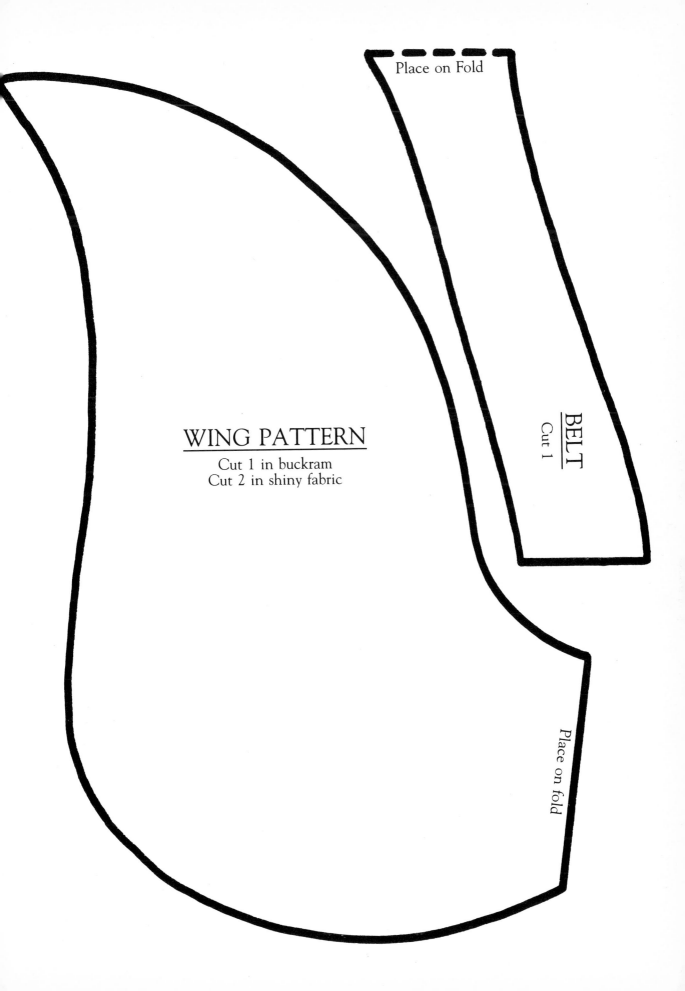

Place on Fold

BELT
Cut 1

WING PATTERN

Cut 1 in buckram
Cut 2 in shiny fabric

Place on fold

CROWN

1 · Cut one from buckram and two from gold fabric. Glue the gold fabric pieces on either side of the buckram. Leave to dry.

2 · Glue gold braid around the bottom edge and around the top pointed edges. Overlap the back edges and glue together.

HAIR

1 · Using pink wool, make the hair as for Hairstyle 1 in the Methods section of Chapter 1. Tie in a pony tail at the back and trim off any excess wool.

2 · When you have finished the hair, glue the crown onto the head.

SLEEVE FRILLS

1 · Cut two pieces of gold net each 12cm (5in) x 3.5cm (1½in).

2 · Gather each piece along one long edge and sew around the top of each arm.

DECORATION

1 · Glue gold braid around the neck edge and wrists.

2 · Using pearl beading, glue around the neck edge forming a loop at the front (Fig 3).

3 · Glue diamante or sequins onto the skirt, crown and body if desired.

Fig 3

WAND

1 · Wrap glittery pink braid around a 20cm (8in) pipecleaner.

2 · Gather a 15cm (6in) × 3.5cm (1½in) piece of gold net on one long edge to form a rosette, glue a glittery button in the middle and glue on top of the wand.

3 · Sew the bottom of the wand to one of the arms.

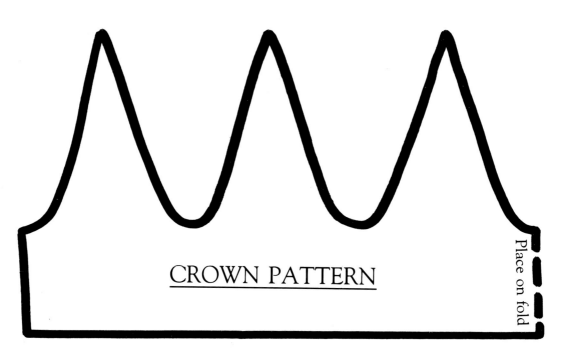

CROWN PATTERN

Place on fold

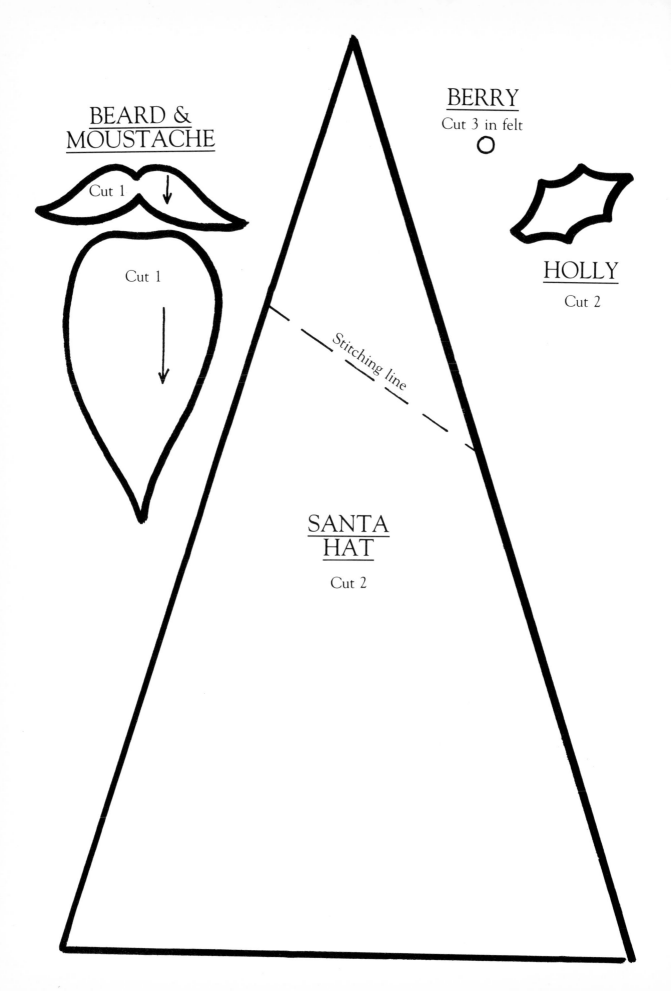

BEARD &
MOUSTACHE

Cut 1

Cut 1

BERRY

Cut 3 in felt

HOLLY

Cut 2

Stitching line

SANTA
HAT

Cut 2

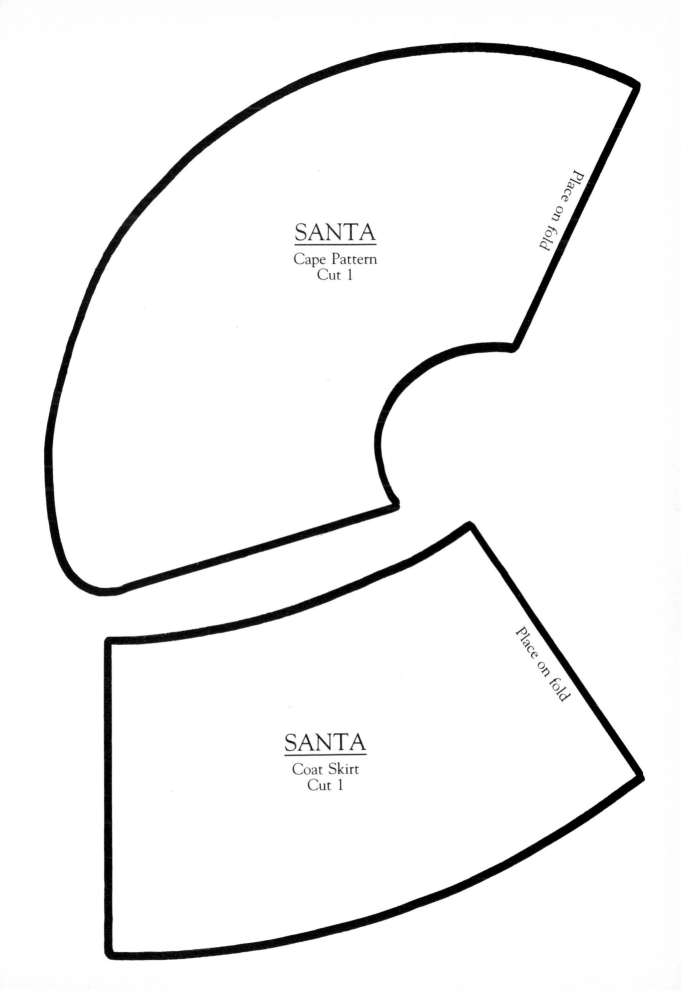

SANTA
Cape Pattern
Cut 1

Place on fold

SANTA
Coat Skirt
Cut 1

Place on fold

SANTA

MATERIALS

1m (38in) × 40cm (16in) of red satin for body, arms, legs, hat, cape and skirt
1m (38in) × 18.5cm (7½in) of white fur fabric for trimmings
20cm (8in) square of long hair fur fabric for the beard
52cm (20½in) × 34cm (13½in) of black felt for boots and belt
Small gold buckle
Scraps of green and red felt for holly
Gold bell
Stuffing

Use Body Pattern 3. For the body, arms and legs use red satin. Use black felt for the boots.

SKIRT

1 · Using the pattern, cut one from red satin.
2 · Cut a piece of white fur fabric 40cm (16in) × 7cm (2½in). Turn in each long edge 1cm (½in) and fold in half lengthways, wrong sides together. Trapping the edge of the skirt in between the fold, bind around the edge stitching through all layers (Fig 1).

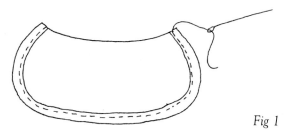

Fig 1

3 · Run a gathering thread around the inner curved edge of the skirt. Place around the waist and stitch in place.

BELT

1 · Cut a piece of black felt 25cm (10in) long and wide enough to fit easily through the buckle.
2 · Sew one end of the belt to the buckle and then fasten the belt around Santa, threading the other end through.

CAPE

1 · Cut one from red satin and bind the curved edges as for the skirt with a piece of white fur fabric 50cm (19½in) × 7cm (2½in).
2 · Gather the inner curved edge to fit around the neck and fasten off securely.

HAT

1 · Cut two from red satin using the pattern. With right sides facing, sew the two long edges together and turn out to the right side.
2 · Cut a piece of white fur fabric 39cm (15½in) × 7cm (2½in) and bind the bottom edge of the hat as for the skirt and cape.
3 · Stitch across the hat as shown by the dotted line on the pattern and sew a bell to the point.
4 · Place a small amount of stuffing in the hat and glue onto the head.
5 · Cut holly and berries from felt using the pattern and glue onto one side of the hat.

BEARD

1 · Cut the beard and moustache from long hair fur fabric using the pattern.
2 · Glue the beard just under the nose and then glue the moustache on top.

DECORATION

For an added festive touch, trim the top of each boot and each wrist with a small strip of fur.

Beach Dolls

Welcome to the beach! This chapter contains a wide range of characters, including a Bathing Beauty, Pirate, Diver and Surfer; it also takes you to a magic kingdom under the sea where you will find my Mermaid and Neptune dolls swimming so happily together beneath the waves!

MERMAID

MATERIALS

60cm (23½in) × 23cm (9in) of flesh calico for the arms and body
40cm (16in) × 30cm (12in) of green shiny fabric for the tail
1m (38in) of lilac braid to trim the tail and waist
50cm (20in) of silver braid for the bra and waist
A bead and a pearl to trim bra
1m (38in) of blue pearl trimming
Diamante trimming or sequins (optional)
Pale green wool

Use Body Pattern 5.

BODY

1 · Cut two body pieces from flesh calico using the body pattern from Body Pattern 3 and cutting along the shorter line as shown on the pattern.

2 · Cut two tail pieces from shiny green fabric using the pattern and remembering to reverse one piece.

3 · With right sides together and raw edges matching, join one tail piece to one body piece (Fig 1). Press the seams open.

4 · Take the other body piece and with right sides facing, place on top of the first. Place the other tail piece on top of the first and tack around the edge leaving a gap in the centre back for turning (Fig 2).

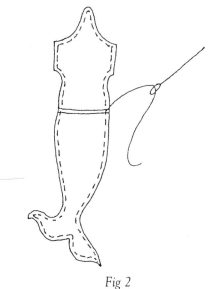

Fig 2

5 · Stitch around the edge and remove the tacking stitches.

6 · Push out to the right side through the gap and stuff firmly pushing right down into the bottom of the tail. Slipstitch the gap together at the back.

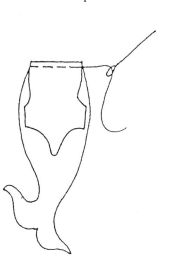

Fig 1

7 · Trim around the edge of the tail by sticking lilac braid around the seam line.

BRA
1 · Cut a piece of silver braid 25cm (10in) long and gather through the centre. Place around the top of the body and overlapping the edges at the back, stitch down.
2 · Sew a bead and a pearl on the front to decorate.

BELT
Cut a piece of silver braid 25cm (10in) long and glue round the waist. Trim around both edges with a 25cm (10in) piece of lilac braid.

ARMS, HEAD AND FACE
Make as described in Body Pattern 5.

HAIR
1 · Using pale green wool, make as described for Hairstyle 1 in the Methods section. Leave the hair long and flowing.
2 · For the bun, cut forty lengths of wool, each 10cm (4in) long. Bunch the ends together and tie with a small piece of wool (Fig 3).

3 · Trim off the ends, puffing out the top into a squashed ball shape.
4 · Glue the bun on top of the head (Fig 4).

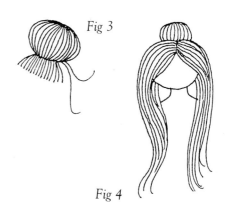

Fig 3

Fig 4

DECORATIONS
1 · Trim the neck edge with blue pearl trimming for a necklace. Tie a small length of the pearl trimming around the wrist for a bracelet.
2 · Decorate the hair with a length of pearl trimming wrapped around the bun and let it flow down each side.
3 · Add a few sequins or diamante on the hair for added glitter.

NEPTUNE

MATERIALS

60cm (23½in) × 23cm (9in) of flesh calico for the arms and body
40cm (16in) × 30cm (12in) of blue shiny fabric for the tail
1m (38in) of narrow green braid to trim the tail and waist
1m (38in) of silver braid for the crown, bracelet and waist
25cm (10in) length of organza
25cm (10in) of sequin trim and a few sequins or diamante for the medallion
Blue/purple wool for the hair and beard
30cm (12in) garden stick, silver ribbon, small piece of buckram and silver fabric
for the trident

Use Body Pattern 5. Make the body, arms, head and belt as for the Mermaid.

HAIR
Using blue/purple wool, make as for Uncle Sam, but trim the ends just below shoulder length.

BEARD
Make the beard as for the Wizard but cut a little shorter.

CROWN
1 · Cut a 25cm (10in) length of silver braid.
2 · Stick the ends together and glue onto the head with the join at the back.

MEDALLION
1 · Cut a 25cm (10in) length of sequin trim.
2 · Cut a 3cm (1in) × 10cm (4in) piece of organza and gather one long edge into a rosette.
3 · Glue a few sequins or diamante in the middle, then glue the rosette onto the centre of the braid.
4 · Glue the medallion around the shoulders, sticking the ends of the sequin trim together at the back.

TRIDENT
1 · Using the prong pattern, cut one from buckram and two from silver fabric.
2 · Glue the silver fabric onto either side of the buckram.
3 · Cover a 30cm (12in) garden stick with silver ribbon and then glue the prong piece on the top of the stick.
4 · Stitch securely to one hand.

PRONG

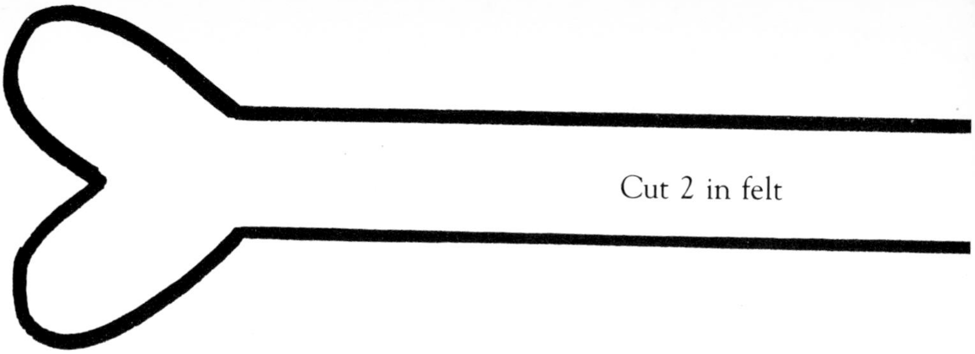

Cut 2 in felt

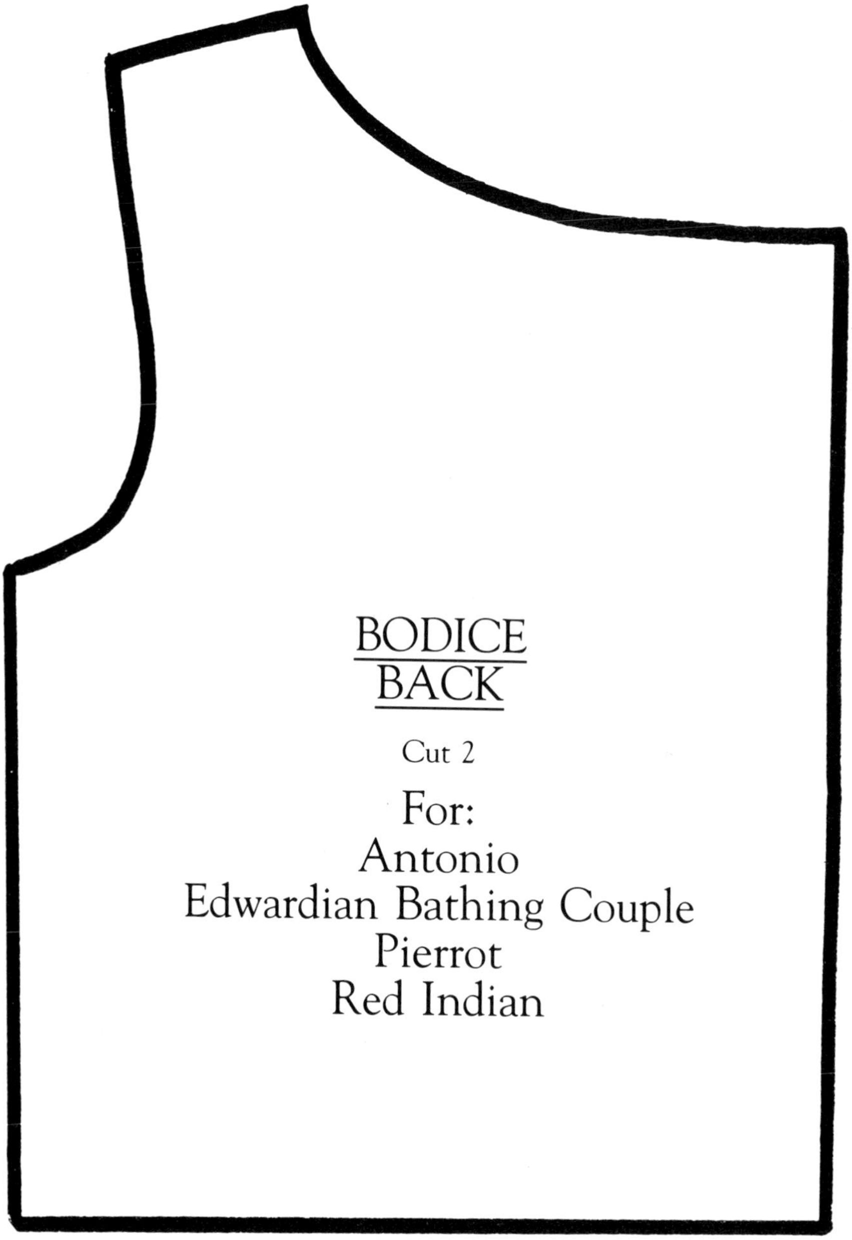

BODICE
BACK

Cut 2

For:
Antonio
Edwardian Bathing Couple
Pierrot
Red Indian

EDWARDIAN BATHING MAN BRACES

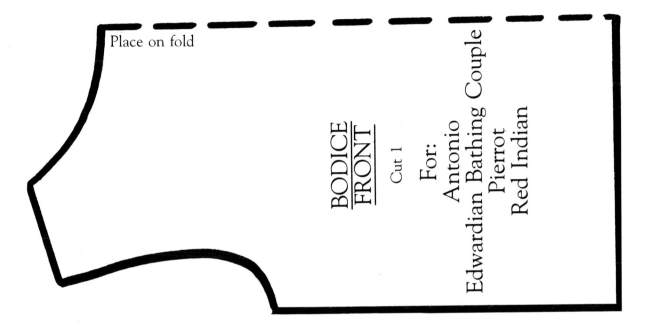

Place on fold

BODICE FRONT

Cut 1

For:
Antonio
Edwardian Bathing Couple
Pierrot
Red Indian

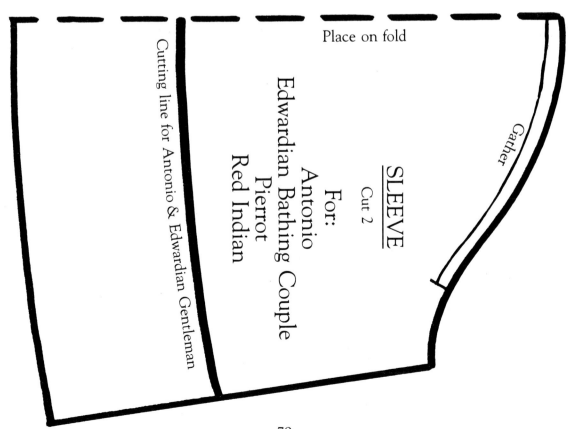

Place on fold

Cutting line for Antonio & Edwardian Gentleman

SLEEVE

Cut 2

For:
Antonio
Edwardian Bathing Couple
Pierrot
Red Indian

Gather

EDWARDIAN BATHING GENTLEMAN

MATERIALS

80cm (31½in) × 50cm (19½in) of blue striped fabric for the trousers and top
1m (38in) length of lemon braid
2 small buttons
30cm (12in) × 12cm (4½in) of red felt for the braces
18cm (7in) square of blue felt for the hanky hat
Yellow wool for the hair and whiskers

Use Body Pattern 2.

BODICE AND TROUSERS

1 · Make from blue striped fabric as for the Edwardian Bathing Lady (overleaf), but cut both sleeves and trouser bottoms shorter as indicated on the pattern. Do not gather the ends of the sleeves and trousers but leave them straight.
2 · Trim the neck edge, sleeves and trouser bottoms with lemon braid.

BRACES

1 · Cut two from red felt using the pattern. Glue two ends onto the inside back of the trousers crossing the braces over (Fig 1).
2 · Bring the other ends over to the front and glue in place onto the top of the trousers (Fig 2).

HAIR

Make as for the Wizard using yellow wool.

WHISKERS

1 · Cut twenty 15cm (6in) lengths of wool. Tie around the middle with a shorter length of wool.
2 · Glue the middle where the mouth would be and stitch the ends under the hair on either side of the face.

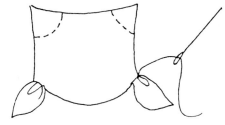

Fig 3

HAT

1 · Cut an 18cm (7in) square of blue felt.
2 · Gather around each corner in a curve 4cm (1½in) from the pointed edge (Fig 3).
3 · Glue onto the head.

TRIMMINGS

Sew two gold anchor buttons to the bodice for an added nautical look.

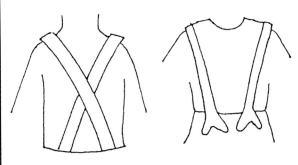

Fig 1   *Fig 2*

EDWARDIAN BATHING LADY

MATERIALS

80cm (31½in) × 50cm (19½in) of pink striped fabric for the trousers and top
52cm (20½in) × 30cm (12in) of pink striped fabric for the mob cap
50cm (19½in) length of blue lace
1.5m (57in) length of white gathered lace
2m (76in) of 4cm (1½in) wide pale blue ribbon
30cm (12in) × 0.5cm (¼in) wide elastic
1m (38in) of narrow pink ribbon
Small blue ribbon bow
Yellow wool for hair

Use Body Pattern 2.

BODICE AND TROUSERS

1 · Make in the same way as the Pierrot (p89) using pink striped fabric, omitting the glittery braid.
2 · Tuck the bodice inside the trousers and trim the neck edge with gathered lace and a bow.

WAISTBAND

1 · Cut a 25cm (10in) length of 4cm (1½in) pale blue ribbon and sew around the waist, overlapping the edges at the back and stitching down.
2 · For the bow, make as for the bow on the Easter Doll following steps 1–3.
3 · Glue the bow on the waist at a slight angle.

HAIR

1 · Make as described in the Methods section using Hairstyle 1 and leave long.
2 · Tie the hair in pony tails on either side of the head with narrow pink ribbon.

MOB CAP

1 · Cut a piece of pink striped fabric 52cm (20½in) × 30cm (12in).

2 · Fold in half lengthways so that it now measures 52cm (20½in) × 15cm (6in).
3 · Stitch blue lace to the folded edge. Stitch a casing 6cm (2½in) from the fold by sewing two lines of stitching 1cm (½in) apart.
4 · Thread elastic through the casing and pull up the elastic so that the mob cap will fit snugly around the head.
5 · Sew the elastic down at each end (Fig 1).

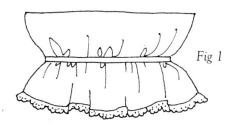

Fig 1

6 · With right sides facing, join the two short edges. Gather the top 1cm (½in) from the edge, pull up the gathers tightly and fasten off.
7 · Glue the mob cap onto the head and decorate the front with a blue bow; make this in the same way as for the bow on the waist but omit the strands.

BATHING BEAUTY

MATERIALS

60cm (23½in) × 25cm (10in) of bright orange satin for the shorts and bikini top
70cm (27½in) × 20cm (8in) of bright pink organza
50cm (19½in) square of print fabric for the hat
50cm (19½in) length of bias binding
2 curtain rings
Gold ribbon
Yellow wool for the hair

Use Body Pattern 2.

SHORTS

1 · Make from orange satin using the trouser pattern, cutting short as indicated on the pattern.
2 · Sew it in the same way as for Uncle Sam hemming the bottom edges.

BIKINI TOP

1 · Cut a 25cm (10in) × 6cm (2½in) strip of orange satin.

Fig 1

2 · Fold the long edges over to meet at the back (Fig 1).
3 · Gather through the middle, pull up the gathers tightly and fasten off (Fig 2).

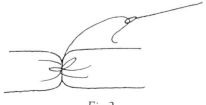

Fig 2

4 · Trim around the middle with a small strip of gold ribbon.
5 · Place around the top of the body, overlap the edges at the back and stitch down.

HAIR

Make from yellow wool as for Hairstyle 1 in the Methods section of Chapter 1 and leave long.

HAT

1 · Using the brim pattern (p86), cut two from print fabric. With wrong sides facing, sew together around the outer and inner edges (Fig 3).

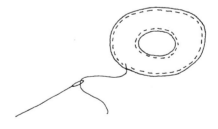

Fig 3

2 · Trim the outer edge with bias binding.
3 · Cut a crown piece (p86) from print fabric and run a gathering thread 1cm (½in) from the edge. Pull up the gathers so that the crown fits around the inner edge of the brim.

4 · With right sides facing, sew the crown to the inner edge (Fig 4).

5 · Glue the hat onto the head.

TRIMMINGS

1 · Cover two wooden curtain rings with gold ribbon and sew on either side of the head for ear-rings.

2 · Cut a 70cm (27½in) × 20cm (8in) piece of bright pink organza, place around the shoulders and tuck under each arm.

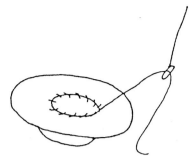

Fig 4

SAMMY SURFER

MATERIALS

60cm (23½in) × 20cm (8in) of bright pink cotton fabric for the shorts
28cm (11in) × 4cm (1½in) of bright pink felt for the headband
40cm (16in) × 10cm (4in) of stiff card for the surfboard
40cm (16in) × 20cm (8in) of lime green felt
Two 13cm (7in) × 1cm (½in) strips of bright pink felt for surfboard
Yellow wool for the hair

Use Body Pattern 2.

SHORTS

Make as for the Bathing Beauty from bright cotton fabric. Cut slightly longer as shown on the trouser pattern.

HAIR

Make as for the Bathing Beauty from yellow wool and cut to shoulder length.

HEADBAND

1 · Cut a strip of bright pink felt 28cm (11in) × 4cm (1½in).

2 · Glue around the head overlapping the edges at the back.

SURFBOARD

1 · Cut a piece of stiff card 40cm (16in) × 10cm (4in) and round off the corners at each end.

2 · Glue lime green felt onto each side.

3 · Decorate by sticking two strips of pink felt each 13cm (7in) × 1cm (½in) across the board at an angle.

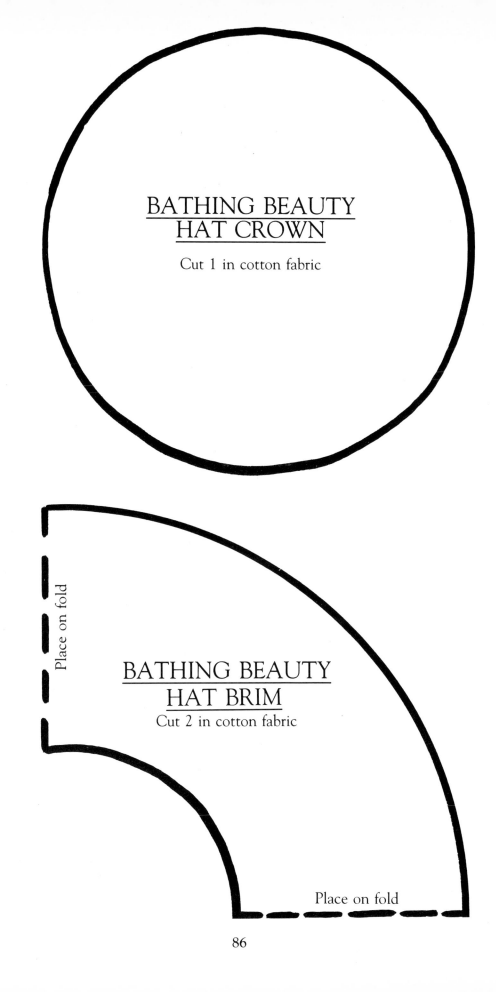

BATHING BEAUTY
HAT CROWN

Cut 1 in cotton fabric

Place on fold

BATHING BEAUTY
HAT BRIM
Cut 2 in cotton fabric

Place on fold

ANTONIO
THE ICE-CREAM SELLER

MATERIALS

60cm (23½in) × 30cm (12in) of red gingham for the trousers
50cm (19½in) square of blue striped fabric for the top
40cm (16in) × 25cm (10in) of white felt for the apron
Small piece of purple felt for the 'A' logo
4cm (1½in) radius circle of pink fur for the ice-cream
22cm (8½in) × 10cm (4in) of buckram for the cone
22cm (8½in) × 10cm (4in) of fawn felt
Small piece of black felt for the moustache
Small piece of brown felt for the flake
Black wool for hair

Use Body Pattern 2.

TROUSERS

Make as for Uncle Sam using red gingham fabric.

SHIRT

Make from blue striped fabric as for the Edwardian Bathing Gentleman using the bodice pattern.

APRON

1 · Cut from white felt using the pattern. For the pocket, cut a 20cm (8in) × 10cm (4in) piece of white felt and sew to the bottom of the apron. Sew down the centre to make a pocket on either side.
2 · Sew a length of ribbon to each corner of the apron at neck and waist.
3 · Using the 'A' logo, cut one from purple felt and glue onto the top of the apron. Fit the apron onto the doll.

HAIR

Make from black wool using Hairstyle 2 as described in the Methods section of Chapter 1.

MOUSTACHE

Cut one from black felt using the pattern and glue onto the face.

ICE-CREAM

1 · Using the cone pattern, cut one from buckram and one from fawn felt. Glue the felt onto the side of the buckram.

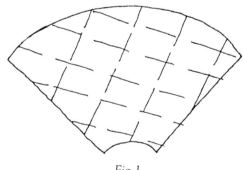

Fig 1

2 · With a brown pencil and a ruler, draw lines diagonally across the cone to give a realistic texture (Fig 1).
3 · Overlap the edges and glue down.

4 · Cut a 4cm (1½in) radius circle from pink fur and gather around the edge, insert a small amount of stuffing and pull up the gathers to form a ball shape. Glue onto the top of the cone.

5 · For the chocolate flake, cut a 4cm (1½in) ×

8cm (3in) piece of brown felt. Spread glue onto one side and roll into the flake shape. Glue on top of the ice-cream.

6 · Sew the ice-cream securely onto one of the hands.

PIERROT

MATERIALS

80cm (31½in) x 50cm (19½in) of white satin for the trousers and top
40cm (16in) × 25cm (10in) of white felt for the hat
5 red pompons
50cm (19½in) × 18cm (7in) of red net for the neck frill
1.5m (57in) of gathered white lace
2m (76in) of glittery red braid
Scrap of red shiny fabric for the hearts on the face

Use Body Pattern 2.

TROUSERS

1 · Make in the same way as for Uncle Sam, following steps 1–4.

2 · Sew gathered white lace around each leg bottom.

3 · When you have fitted the trousers onto the doll, gather each leg 4cm (1½in) from the bottom edge. Pull up the gathers and fasten off securely. Repeat for the other leg.

4 · Glue glittery red braid around the gathers to cover up the stitching.

BODICE

1 · Make in the same way as for the Downhill Skier's jumper using white satin and following steps 1–4.

2 · Sew gathered lace and glittery braid onto the bottom edge of the bodice and each sleeve. Fit onto the doll.

3 · Run a gathering thread 2cm (1in) from the

bottom edge of each sleeve. Pull up the gathers tightly and fasten off. Trim the gathers with glittery braid.

4 · Glue two pompons onto the front of the bodice.

NECK FRILL

1 · Cut three pieces of red net each 60cm (23½in) × 10cm (4in).

2 · Gather along one long edge through all layers. Place around the neck, pull up the gathers and fasten off. Trim around the neck edge with glittery braid.

HAT

1 · Make as for Santa but use white felt and glue glittery braid to the bottom edge instead of fur.

2 · Glue two pompons onto the centre of the hat and a pompon onto the pointed end.

TRIMMINGS

For an added touch, cut two small hearts from shiny red fabric and glue on either side of the mouth.

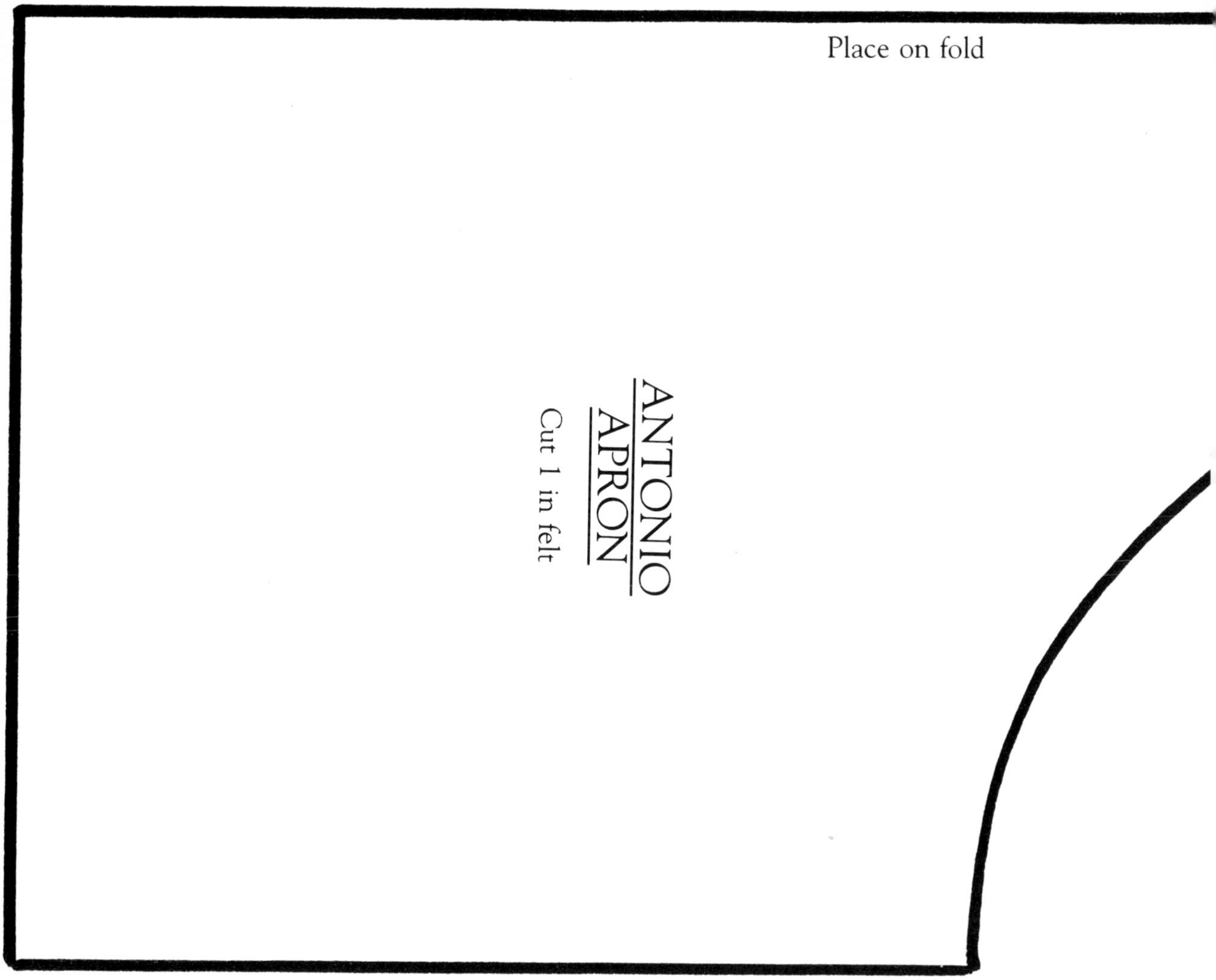

Place on fold

ANTONIO
APRON

Cut 1 in felt

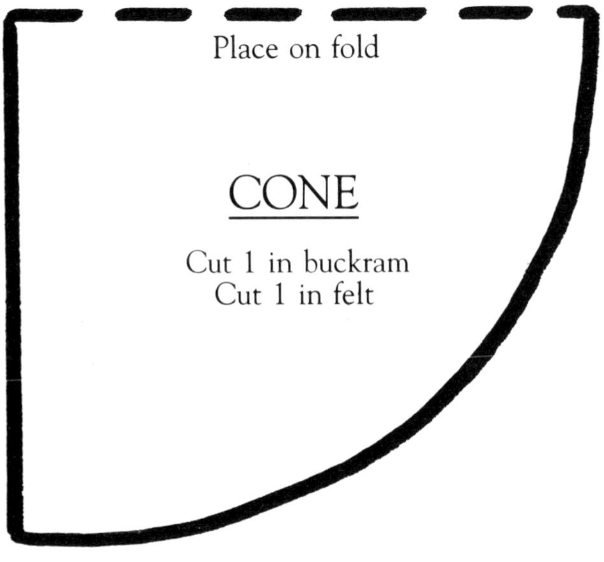

Place on fold

CONE

Cut 1 in buckram
Cut 1 in felt

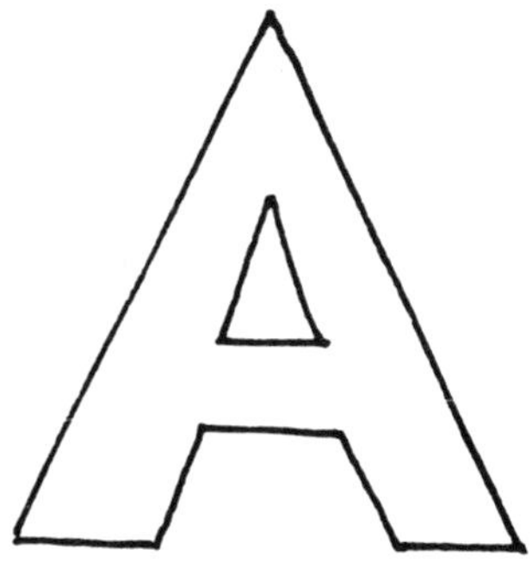

A

LOGO FOR ANTONIO

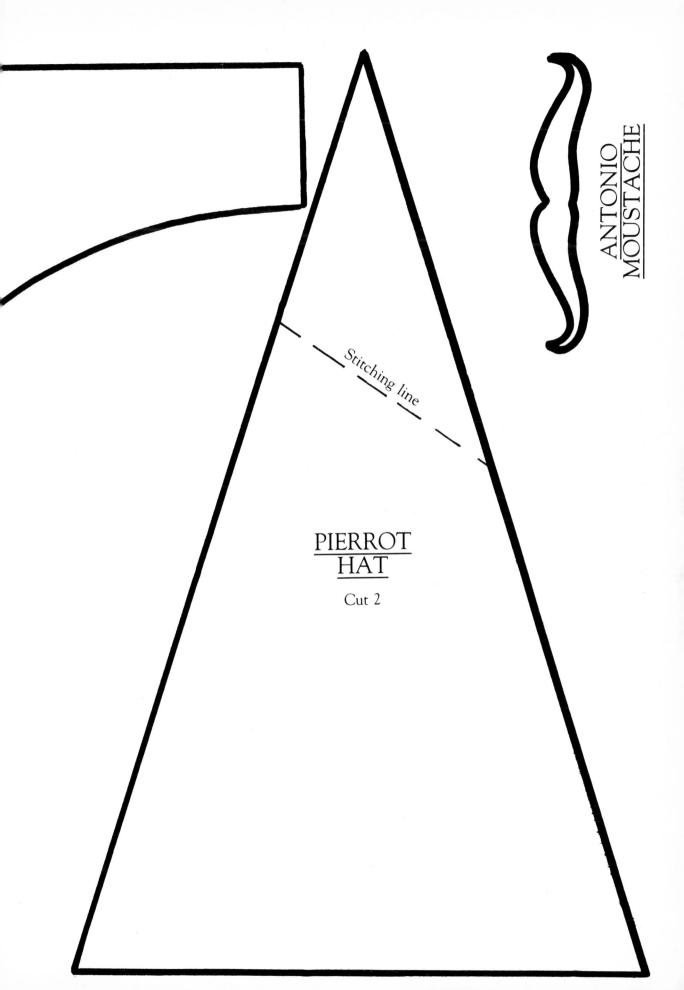

ANTONIO
MOUSTACHE

Stitching line

PIERROT
HAT

Cut 2

DIVER

MATERIALS

1m (38in) × 40cm (16in) of flesh calico
40cm (16in) × 30cm (12in) of blue felt for the flippers, mask and snorkel
30cm (12in) square of blue satin for shorts
50cm (19½in) × 25cm (9½in) of purple felt for the oxygen cylinders
40cm (16in) × 30cm (12in) of buckram for the flippers, snorkel and oxygen cylinders
30cm (12in) length of plastic piping (the sort used for winemaking)
1m (38in) of silver ric-rac braid
20cm (8in) length of green velvet ribbon
8cm (3in) length of shiny braid for the watch
Small scraps of silver and red shiny fabric for the belt decoration and the watch
Brown wool for the hair

Use Body Pattern 3. Make the arms, hands, body, legs and feet from flesh calico.

SHORTS

Make from blue satin as for the Bathing Beauty and trim the edges with silver ric-rac braid.

HAIR

Make from brown wool using Hairstyle 2 as described in the Methods section of Chapter 1.

BODICE DECORATION

1 · Glue two strips of silver ric-rac braid from the back of the doll, over the shoulders and tapering into the waist.
2 · Glue a small strip of braid across the top. Cover the raw ends of the braid by sticking a 25cm (9½in) length of green velvet ribbon around the waist edge.

OXYGEN CYLINDERS

1 · Using the pattern, cut one from buckram and two from purple felt. Sew the purple felt onto each side of the buckram.
2 · Glue or sew the oxygen cylinders onto the back of the doll securely.

MASK AND SNORKEL

1 · Cut a mask from blue felt and glue just above the nose.
2 · Cut a snorkel from buckram and blue felt. Glue the felt onto one side of the buckram. Glue onto the doll where the mouth should be.
3 · Cut a 30cm (12in) length of piping and sew the middle just under the snorkel taking the ends over to the back of the doll.

FLIPPERS

1 · Using the pattern, cut two from buckram and two from blue felt.
2 · For each flipper, glue a piece of felt on either side of the buckram and sew around the edge.
3 · Sew along the three dotted lines on each flipper.
4 · Glue or sew a flipper onto each ankle.

TRIMMINGS

1 · Sew a piece of shiny braid around the wrist and a small circle of shiny red fabric on top to look like an underwater watch.
2 · Glue a small silver fabric circle onto the front of the waist to finish.

DIVER
OXYGEN CYLINDERS

Cut 1 in buckram
Cut 2 in felt

Place on fold

MASK FOR DIVER

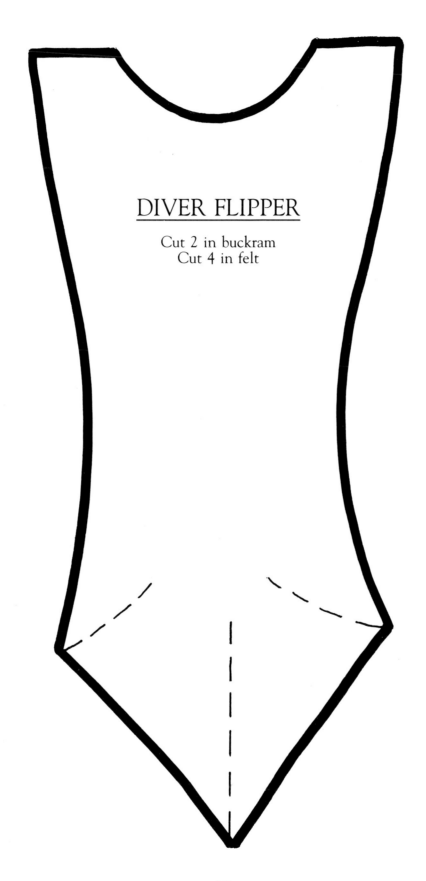

DIVER FLIPPER

Cut 2 in buckram
Cut 4 in felt

PIRATE

MATERIALS

70cm (27½in) × 30cm (12in) of black felt for the boots, hat and eyepatch
Small piece of white felt for the skull and crossbones
30cm (12in) × 25cm (9½in) of buckram for the hat
32cm (12½in) × 12cm (4½in) of red/white striped fabric for the legs
55cm (21½in) × 30cm (12in) of cream satin for the body and sleeves
50cm (19½in) × 25cm (9½in) of flesh calico for the arms and hands
40cm (16in) × 30cm (12in) of burgundy felt for the coat
1m (38in) of gold braid
1m (38in) of cream lace
18cm (7in) × 5cm (2in) of buckram for the scabbard
18cm (7in) × 10cm (4in) of silver fabric for the scabbard
25cm (9½in) × 2cm (1in) of brown felt for the belt
12cm (7in) length of gold ribbon

Use Body Pattern 3. Cut the arms from flesh calico, the legs from red/white striped fabric, the boots from black felt and the body from cream satin.

SLEEVES

1 · Cut two pieces of cream satin each 24cm (9½in) × 20cm (8in) and hem one long edge 4cm (1½in) on each piece.
2 · With right sides facing, join the short edges and turn out to the right side.
3 · Hem the other long edge 1cm (½in) on each piece and gather around the shoulders. Gather the 3cm (1½in) hemmed edge around the wrists 2cm (1in) from the edge to form a frill.
4. · Cut two 15cm (6in) lengths of cream lace and gather around each wrist for an extra frill.

COAT

1 · Cut one back and two front pieces from burgundy felt, remembering to reverse one front piece. With right sides facing join at the shoulder seams.
2 · Cut two epaulettes from felt and, with right sides facing, sew the inner curved edge of each epaulette to both armholes (Fig 1).

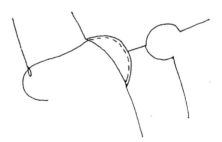

Fig 1

3 · With right sides together, join the side seams of the coat.
4 · Glue gold braid around the two front edges and around the bottom edge of the coat.
5 · Fit the coat onto the doll; you may need to bend the arms slightly to do this.

NECK FRILL

1 · Cut a 6cm (2½in) and a 10cm (4in) piece of cream lace. Gather along the long edge of both pieces and fasten off to make two semi-circular rosettes.

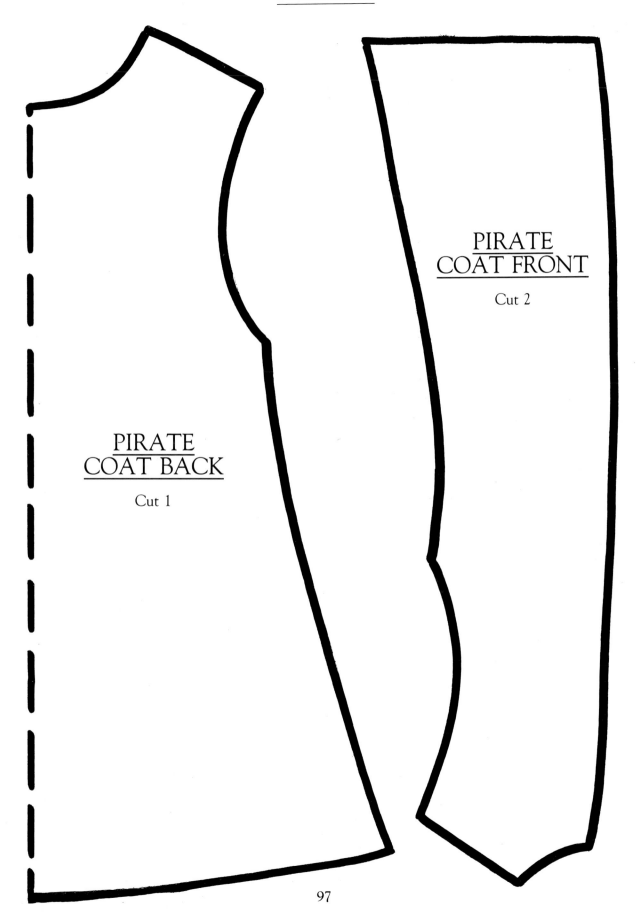

PIRATE
COAT FRONT

Cut 2

PIRATE
COAT BACK

Cut 1

PIRATE HAT

Cut 2 in buckram

PIRATE EPAULETTE

Cut 2

2 · Glue the small one on top of the larger one then glue both at the neck edge.

EYEPATCH

1 · Cut from black felt using the pattern and glue onto the centre of a 12cm (7in) length of gold ribbon.

Pirate Eyepatch

2 · Glue onto the face over one eye at an angle so that the gold ribbon covers half of the head.

HAT

1 · Cut two in buckram using the pattern and cover both sides of each piece with black felt.
2 · Using the skull and crossbones pattern, cut from white felt and glue onto one side of the hat.
3 · Glue both hat pieces together on the head pressing the ends firmly together.

SCABBARD

1 · Cut one from buckram and two from silver fabric.
2 · Glue the silver fabric onto either side of the buckram.
3 · Sew the scabbard onto one hand.

BELT

Cut a 25cm (9½in) × 2cm (1in) strip of brown felt and glue around the waist.

TRIMMINGS

1 · Trim the top of each boot by cutting two pieces of black felt each 13cm (5in) × 6cm (2½in).
2 · Wrap around the top of each boot overlapping the edges at the back and slipstitching together to finish.

SCABBARD

Costume Dolls

Dressing dolls in costume provides endless scope for experimenting with exotic fabrics and trimmings. Simply researching historical costume can prove fascinating; looking at old paintings and books for the correct details needed for a specific look can give hours of pleasure. This chapter has a large selection of costume dolls to choose from and who knows, it may even inspire you to create a whole collection!

ELIZABETHAN DOLL

MATERIALS

1m (38in) square of glittery fabric for body, arms, sleeves, skirt and hip frill
80cm (32in) × 33cm (13in) of purple satin for the underskirt
40cm (16in) × 20cm (8in) of buckram for the butterfly collar and stomacher
30cm (12in) × 20cm (8in) of gold net for the butterfly collar
35cm (14in) × 10cm (4in) of gold fabric for the stomacher
1m (38in) of white gathered lace
4m (152in) of gold braid
50cm (19½in) of glittery pink braid
50cm (19½in) of narrow purple braid
10 pink satin bows
35cm (14in) × 10cm (4in) of white organza for the ruff
20cm (8in) of pearl trimmings and a large purple pearl bead for the headdress
Mustard coloured wool for hair

Use Body Pattern 1.

SKIRT

1 · Cut a piece of purple satin for the underskirt 80cm (32in) × 33cm (13in). Hem one long straight edge 1cm (½in) and sew gathered lace to this edge.
2 · With right sides facing, join the short edges together and turn out to the right side.
3 · Gather 1cm (½in) from the top to fit around the waist.
4 · Cut a piece of glittery fabric 80cm (32in) × 33cm (13in). Hem three edges and sew gold braid to them.
5 · Gather the remaining long edge around the waist with the opening at the front. Sew five pink bows down each side.

HIP FRILL

1 · Cut a piece of glittery fabric 60cm (23½in) × 20cm (8in).
2 · Fold in half along the length and gather along the raw edges around the waist with the ends at the back. Fasten off securely.

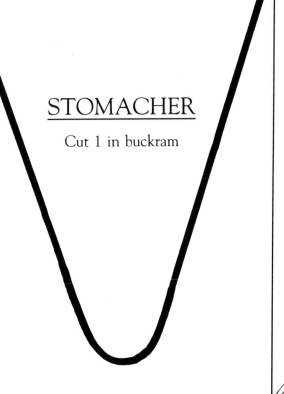

STOMACHER

Cut 1 in buckram

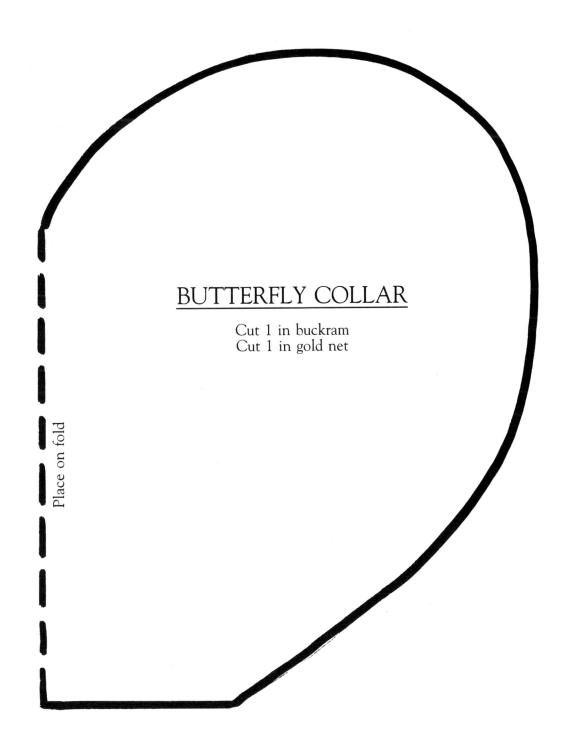

BUTTERFLY COLLAR

Cut 1 in buckram
Cut 1 in gold net

Place on fold

SLEEVES

Make in the same way as for the Queen of Hearts using glittery fabric.

STOMACHER

1 · Make in the same way as for the Queen of Hearts but use gold fabric to cover the buckram.
2 · Glue purple braid in a criss-cross fashion across the front.
3 · Trim around the edge with glittery pink braid and glue onto the doll.

RUFF

1 · Cut a piece of white organza 35cm (14in) × 10cm (4in).
2 · Fold in half along the length and gather along the raw edge, pulling up the gathers to fit around the neck with the open edges at the back.

HAIR

Using mustard coloured wool, make as for Hairstyle 1 in the Methods section of Chapter 1 and tie at the back trimming off the excess wool.

HEADDRESS

1 · Sew a 20cm (8in) length of pearl trimming around the head, sewing the ends together at the back.
2 · Sew a purple bead on the front.

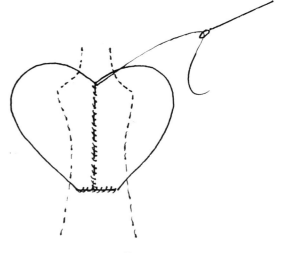

Fig 1

BUTTERFLY COLLAR

1 · Cut one from buckram and one from gold net. Sew the gold net onto one side of the buckram.
2 · Trim the edge with white gathered lace.
3 · Using a large darning needle, sew onto the back of the doll (Fig 1).

TRIMMINGS

Trim around each cuff with gathered white lace for a finishing touch.

VICTORIAN MISS

MATERIALS

25cm (9½in) × 40cm (16in) of flesh calico for the arms and hands
1m (38in) square of shiny tartan fabric for the upper body and dress
4m (152in) of cream lace
50cm (19½in) of green velvet ribbon
2 small bunches of artificial flowers
25cm (9½in) × 8cm (3in) of buckram
30cm (12in) × 12cm (5in) of green satin
50cm (19½in) of blue pearl trimming
2 glittery beads and a small strip of blue ribbon for the choker
35cm (14in) of 8cm (3in) wide burgundy lace
Brown wool for hair

Use Body Pattern 1. Make the arms from flesh calico and the upper body from tartan fabric.

SKIRT

1 · Cut a piece of tartan fabric 80cm (32in) × 30cm (12in), a piece 80cm (32in) × 24cm (9½in) and a piece 80cm (32in) × 16cm (6½in).
2 · Hem one long edge 1cm (½in) on all pieces and sew cream lace to this edge on all pieces.
3 · With right sides facing, join the short edges together on all pieces. Turn out to the right side and matching the top raw edges, fit one piece inside another with the smallest piece at the top and the longest at the bottom.
4 · Gather the top edge around the waist and fasten off securely.

BELT

Make as for the Christmas Fairy but cover the buckram with green satin.

NECK FRILL

1 · Cut a 60cm (23½in) × 6cm (2½in) piece of tartan fabric. Hem one long edge 1cm (½in) and sew cream lace to this edge.
2 · Hem the other edge 1cm (½in) and with right sides facing, join the short edges. Turn out to the right side and gather around the shoulders. Pull up the gathers and fasten off.
3 · Sew cream lace around the inner edge of the frill.

HAIR

1 · Make from brown wool as described for Hairstyle 1 in the Methods section of Chapter 1.
2 · Tie at the back and tuck the ends under.

HAIR DECORATION

1 · Sew a loop of velvet ribbon and a small bunch of flowers onto either side of the head.
2 · Cut a 35cm (14in) piece of burgundy lace 8cm (3in) wide, gather along one long edge into a rosette and glue onto the back of the head.

DECORATIONS

Sew blue ribbon and two beads at the neck for a choker. Sew blue pearl trimming to each wrist for bracelets.

EDWARDIAN LADY

MATERIALS

1m (38in) square of pink satin for the underskirt, arms and upper body
1m (38in) square of pink organza for the overskirt, puff sleeves and hat decoration
30cm (12in) × 20cm (8in) of buckram for the hat
1m (38in) × 40cm (16in) of pink satin for the hat
25cm (9½in) × 8cm (3in) of buckram
30cm (12in) × 12cm (4½in) of pink/white striped fabric
3m (114in) of white gathered lace
70cm (27½in) length of marabou feather trim
Small pieces of bright pink organza and pink marabou feather trim for the hat
Cream wool for hair

Use Body Pattern 1. Make the upper body and arms from pink satin.

SKIRT
Make from pink satin and pink organza in the same way as for the Easter Parade Doll following steps 1–4. Trim the bottom edge of the organza overskirt with white gathered lace.

BELT
Make as for the Christmas Fairy and cover the buckram with pink/white striped fabric.

SLEEVES
Make in the same way as for the Queen of Hearts following steps 1–4. Instead of the red braid, use white gathered lace.

HAIR
Make as for the Easter Parade Doll using cream wool.

HAT
1 · Make as for the Easter Parade Doll following steps 1–4 and using pink satin.
2 · Trim the top by ruffling pink organza around the brim. For added decoration, sew on two short pieces of marabou feather.

TRIMMINGS
1 · Trim the wrists with white gathered lace.
2 · Cut a 70cm (27½in) length of marabou and place around the arms, stitching in place.

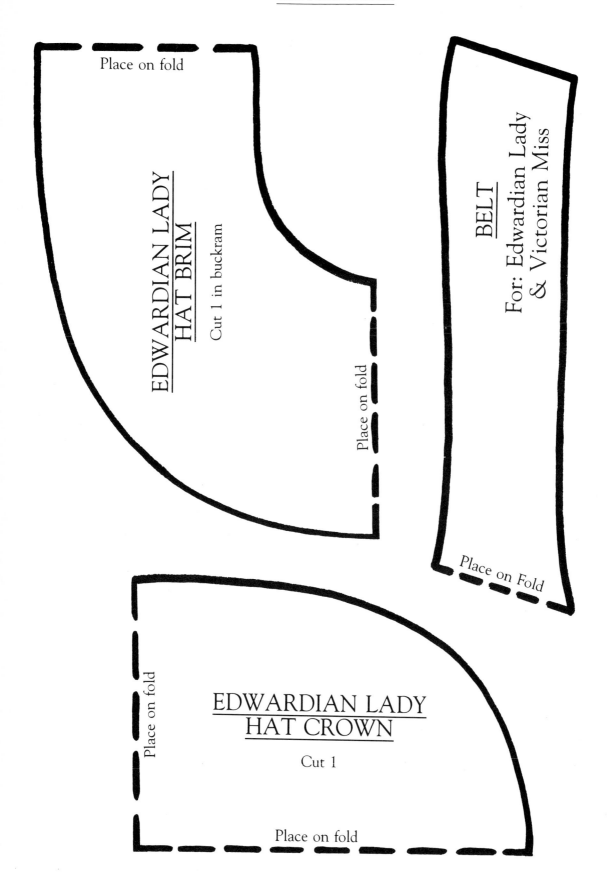

Place on fold

EDWARDIAN LADY
HAT BRIM

Cut 1 in buckram

Place on fold

BELT

For: Edwardian Lady
& Victorian Miss

Place on Fold

Place on fold

EDWARDIAN LADY
HAT CROWN

Cut 1

Place on fold

1920's FLAPPER

MATERIALS

30cm (12in) × 25cm (9½in) of lilac satin for the body
80cm (32in) × 25cm (9½in) of flesh calico for the hands, arms and legs
40cm (16in) × 12cm (5in) of white felt for the shoes
1m (38in) × 70cm (27½in) of non-fray lilac chiffon
1m (38in) × 70cm (27½in) of non-fray blue chiffon
25cm (9½in) of 5cm (2in) wide lilac ribbon for the waistband
20cm (8in) × 10cm (4in) of lilac satin and a glittery button for the waist decoration
30cm (12in) length of silver braid and 2 feathers for the headdress
50cm (19½in) of purple sequin trimming
Scraps of lilac braid for the bracelets
Beading for the necklace
Brown wool for hair

Use Body Pattern 3. Make the arms and legs from flesh calico, the shoes from white felt and the body from lilac satin.

SKIRT

1 · Cut six 35cm (14in) squares of lilac chiffon and six 35cm (14in) squares of blue chiffon.
2 · Pinch the centre of each square and sew around the top of the legs alternating the colours.

WAISTBAND

1 · Wrap a 25cm (9½in) length of 5cm (2in) wide lilac ribbon around the waist, overlapping the edges at the back and stitching down. Trim the edges with purple sequin trimming.
2 · Cut a 20cm (8in) × 10cm (4in) strip of lilac satin. Fold in half lengthways and gather along the raw edges into a rosette.
3 · Glue a glittery button in the centre and then glue the rosette on one side of the waistband.

SLEEVES

1 · Cut four 10cm (4in) squares of lilac chiffon and two 10cm (4in) squares of blue chiffon.
2 · Take two lilac squares and a blue square then sew together on each arm.

HAIR

1 · Make the basic hairstyle using brown wool as for Hairstyle 1 from the Methods section of Chapter 1, tucking the ends under at the back.
2 · Glue silver braid around the forehead for a headband.
3 · Cut fifteen pieces of wool each 50cm (19½in) long. Tie together at one end and plait. Tie at the end and then sew into a coil (Fig 1). Repeat for the other coil.

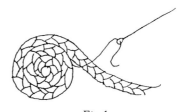

Fig 1

4 · Glue the coils on either side of the head.
5 · Glue two feathers on the side of the headband to finish off the headdress.

DECORATION

Sew lilac braid around the wrists for bracelets and beading around the neck for a necklace.

RED INDIAN

MATERIALS

*80cm (32in) × 50cm (19½in) of fawn fleece
fabric for the trousers and top
70cm (27½in) of lilac braid
35cm (14in) of lemon braid
45cm (18in) of cream braid
15 assorted small feathers
25cm (9½in) length of green velvet ribbon
Brown wool for hair*

Use Body Pattern 2 and a darker coloured calico.

TROUSERS AND TOP

1 · Make the trousers from fawn fleece in the same way as for Uncle Sam, but do not hem the bottom edge; cut at intervals for a ragged edge.

2 · Make the top from fawn fleece in the same way as the Downhill Skier. Do not hem the bottom and the sleeve ends, but cut at intervals as for trousers. Trim the neck edge with lilac braid.

HAIR

1 · Make from brown wool following Hairstyle 1 in the Methods section of Chapter 1, leaving the hair long. Make two plaits on either side of the head using fifteen strands of wool on each side.

2 · Trim the ends with lemon braid.

HEADDRESS

1 · Glue a piece of green velvet ribbon around the head and glue feathers to the top inside edge.

3 · Cut two 22.5 (9in) lengths of cream braid and glue four feathers near one end on each piece.

3 · Glue this end on both pieces to either side of the head to finish.

SPANISH SENORITA

MATERIALS

60cm (23½in) × 30cm (12in) of black taffeta for the upper body and arms
80cm (32in) × 40cm (16in) of non-fray pink organza
80cm (32in) × 32cm (12½in) of non-fray lime organza
80cm (32in) × 33cm (13in) of non-fray black organza
50cm (19½in) of glittery red braid
20cm (8in) of 5cm (2in) wide glittery red braid for the waist
70cm (27½in) of 10cm (4in) wide black lace
10cm (4in) square of buckram
20cm (8in) × 10cm (4in) piece of black felt
15cm (6in) × 10cm (4in) of buckram, small piece of white lace, gold ribbon and a red bow
for the fan
Red fabric rose for the hair decoration
Brown wool for hair

Use Body Pattern 1. Make the arms and upper body from black taffeta.

SKIRT
1 · Cut a piece of black organza 80cm (32in) × 33cm (13in), a piece of lime organza 80cm (32in) × 24cm (9in) and a piece of pink organza 80cm (32in) × 16cm (6½in).
2 · With the black piece at the bottom, the lime piece in the middle and the pink piece on top, place the long raw edges together and gather around the waist (Fig 1).

Fig 1

3 · Sew a 20cm (8in) piece of 5cm (2in) wide glittery red braid around the waist.

NECK FRILL
1 · Cut a piece of pink organza 60cm (23½in) × 5cm (2in), a piece 60cm (23½in) × 10cm (4in) and a piece of lime organza 60cm (23½in) × 8cm (3in).
2 · With the lime organza inbetween the two pink pieces, match up the long edges and gather around the neck, stitching through all layers.
3 · Glue glittery braid around the neck.

WRIST FRILLS
1 · Cut two pieces of pink organza each 4cm (1½in) × 12cm (5in) and gather one long edge around each wrist.
2 · Trim the top edge with glittery braid.

HAIR
Make from black wool as described for Hairstyle 1 in the Methods section of Chapter 1. Tie at the back, trim off the excess wool and tuck the ends under.

HEADDRESS

1 · Using the pattern, cut one from buckram and glue black felt onto both sides. Trim the edges with red glittery braid.

2 · Cut two 35cm (13½in) × 10cm (4in) pieces of black lace and glue the ends of each piece onto the bottom of the headdress.

3 · Glue the headdress onto the head.

4 · Stick a red fabric rose onto the side of the head for an added decorative touch.

FAN

1 · Cut one from buckram and cover with lace.

2 · Sew three loops of gold ribbon and a red bow to the pointed end.

3 · Stitch the fan securely onto a hand.

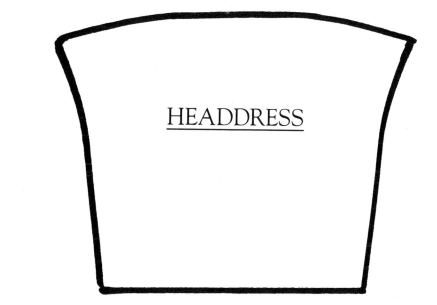

HEADDRESS

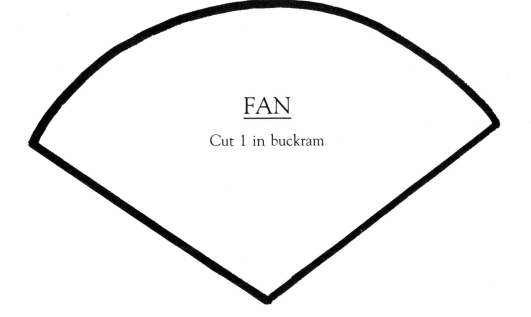

FAN

Cut 1 in buckram

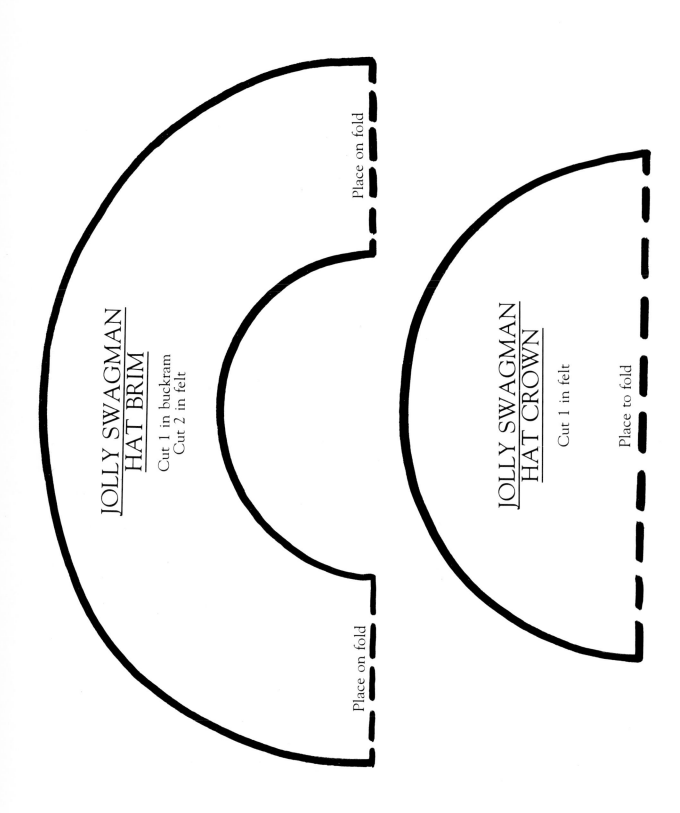

JOLLY SWAGMAN
HAT BRIM

Cut 1 in buckram
Cut 2 in felt

Place on fold

Place on fold

JOLLY SWAGMAN
HAT CROWN

Cut 1 in felt

Place to fold

JOLLY SWAGMAN

MATERIALS

32cm (12½in) × 12cm (5in) of fawn corduroy for the trousers
70cm (27½in) × 30cm (12in) of checked fabric for the body and arms
30cm (12in) × 20cm (8in) of brown corduroy for the waistcoat
70cm (27½in) × 18cm (7in) of brown felt for the boots
1m (38in) of lemon braid
20cm (8in) × 10cm (4in) of rust felt for the corks
60cm (23½in) × 20cm (8in) of brown felt for the hat
20cm (8in) square of buckram
25cm (9½in) length of mustard velvet ribbon
Yellow wool for hair

Use Body Pattern 3. Make the arms and body from checked fabric, the boots from brown felt and the legs from fawn corduroy. Trim around top of boots with mustard velvet ribbon.

WAISTCOAT

1 · Cut from brown corduroy and make in the same way as for Uncle Sam omitting the glittery sequins.
2 · Trim around the edge with lemon braid.

HAIR

1 · Make as for the Wizard using yellow wool.
2 · The moustache is made from fifteen pieces of wool each 15cm (6in) long. Tie in the middle with a small length of wool and glue just under the nose letting the wool flop down.

HAT

1 · Using the brim pattern, cut one from buckram and two from brown felt. Glue the felt on either side of the buckram.
2 · Cut a crown from brown felt and stitch to the inner edge of the brim as for the Bathing Beauty.
3 · For the corks, cut ten pieces of rust felt each 10cm (4in) × 2cm (1in). Spread glue on one side and roll up tightly as for Antonio's flake.
4 · Using strong thread, knot one end and thread through the centre of a cork, sew onto the edge of the hat. Sew the other corks in the same way all around the hat.
5 · Glue the hat onto the head to finish.

GENIE MOUSTACHE

Gather around the curved edge

WAISTCOAT BACK

Cut 1

For: Jolly Swagman
& Genie

Place on fold

WAISTCOAT FRONT

For: Jolly Swagman
& Genie

(dotted line indicates
cutting line for Genie)

GENIE TURBAN

Cut 1 in shiny fabric

GENIE

MATERIALS

80cm (32in) × 25cm (9½in) of flesh calico for the arms and legs
60cm (23½in) × 30cm (12in) of gold/pink striped fabric for the trousers
40cm (16in) × 12cm (5in) of lime satin for the shoes
1.5m (57in) of glittery purple braid
Two 30cm (12in) pipecleaners
30cm (12in) length of gold braid
30cm (12in) × 20cm (8in) of shiny blue fabric for the waistcoat
55cm (21½in) × 30cm (12in) of glittery pink fabric for the body and sleeves
26cm (10in) × 20cm (8in) of glittery green fabric for the turban
Small amount of stuffing
10cm (4in) × 2cm (1in) of bright pink organza, a small purple feather and a large bead for the turban
Purple felt for the moustache and beard
28cm (11in) length of silver ric-rac braid
10cm (4in) × 2cm (1in) of bright pink organza and a glittery button for the medallion

The character of this doll lies in the choice of rich, glittery fabrics you use for the clothes and trimmings. Bright, shimmering lamé fabrics and brocades will help to create the illusion that he has just appeared out of a magic lamp!

Use Body Pattern 3. Make the body from pink glittery fabric, the shoes from lime satin and the legs and arms from flesh calico.

TROUSERS

1 · Using the trouser pattern, cut from gold/pink striped fabric and make as for Uncle Sam.
2 · Gather the bottom edge around the ankles and fasten off securely. Trim around the ankles with glittery purple braid.

SLEEVES

1 · From glittery pink fabric, cut two pieces each 20cm (8in) × 17cm (7in).
2 · Hem the short edges on both pieces and with right sides facing, join the long edges and then push out to the right side.

3 · Place a sleeve on each arm and gather to fit around the shoulders and wrists. Fasten off securely.

WAISTCOAT

1 · Cut from shiny blue fabric, cutting along the dotted line on the pattern for the front pieces.
2 · Make as for Uncle Sam omitting the trimmings.

MEDALLION

1. · Glue a strip of silver ric-rac braid around the neck into a point at the front.
2 · Cut a 10cm (4in) × 2cm (1in) piece of pink organza and gather along one long edge into a rosette. Glue a glittery button in the middle and glue onto the pointed end of the ric-rac braid.

MOUSTACHE AND BEARD

Cut from purple felt using the moustache pattern. Use the beard pattern from Santa. Glue onto the face.

COSTUME DOLLS

TURBAN

1 · Cut one from glittery green fabric using the pattern. Gather along the curved edge onto the head. Insert a small amount of stuffing. Pull up the gathers tightly and fasten off (Fig 1).

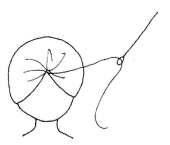

Fig 1

2 · Glue a feather to the centre. Make a rosette as for the medallion and glue this on top of the feather. Sew a large bead on the front.

DECORATIONS

1 · Trim the neck edge with gold braid.
2 · For the Turkish slippers, glue purple braid to two 30cm (12in) pipecleaners.
3 · Bend in half and with the fold at the back, glue around the bottom of each shoe and glue the ends together. Bend both ends into a curl (Fig 2).

Fig 2

EASTERN PRINCESS

MATERIALS

60cm (23½in) × 30cm (12in) of purple organza for the trousers
10cm (4in) × 5cm (2in) of glittery fabric for the bra
40cm (16in) × 20cm (8in) of purple organza for the sleeves
25cm (9½in) × 7cm (3in) of glittery lilac fabric for the waistband
40cm (16in) × 28cm (11in) of lilac organza for the veil
Mother-of-pearl sequins, glittery beads and braids as desired to trim the doll

Use Body Pattern 2.

TROUSERS

Using the trouser pattern, cut two front pieces and two back pieces from purple organza. Make as for Uncle Sam and gather the bottom edge around the ankles.

BRA

Using purple glittery fabric, make as for the Bathing Beauty bikini top. Trim with a bead.

WAISTBAND

1 · Cut one from glittery fabric, trim the edges with gold beading and sew around the waist.
2 · Sew beads around the edge of the waistband.

SLEEVES

1 · Cut two 20cm (8in) × 10cm (4in) pieces of purple organza.
2 · With right sides facing, join the short edges and turn out to the right side.

3 · Hem the raw edges and gather both edges on each sleeve around the bottom of each arm.
4 · Trim the edges with glittery braid.

HAIR

Using black wool, make as for Hairstyle 1 in the Methods section of Chapter 1, leave the hair long.

HEADDRESS AND VEIL

1 · Glue a length of pearl beading around the head.
2 · Gather one long edge of a 40cm (16in) × 28cm (11in) piece of lilac organza and sew onto the back of the head.

TRIMMINGS

1 · Glue some mother-of-pearl sequins onto the trousers for added glitter.
2 · Glue gold braid around the arms for bracelets.
3 · Sew a bead onto the front of the headdress and two beads on either side of the head for earrings.

SPACE HERO

MATERIALS

80cm (32in) × 50cm (19½in) of glittery pink fabric for the cape, belt and boots
35cm (14in) × 30cm (12in) of silver fabric for the arms, mask and gauntlets
1.5m (57in) of silver braid
60cm (23½in) × 30cm (12in) of shiny green fabric for the body and legs
45cm (18in) of 2.5cm (1in) wide glittery green braid
30cm (12in) × 23cm (9½in) of buckram
1m (38in) of silver ric-rac braid
1m (38in) of silver ribbon
30cm (12in) × 24cm (10in) black felt
4 shiny beads
Mustard coloured wool for hair

Use Body Pattern 3. Make the body and legs from green shiny fabric, the boots from bright pink shiny fabric and the arms from silver fabric.

GAUNTLETS

1 · Using the pattern cut one from buckram and one from silver fabric. Glue the silver fabric onto one side of the buckram.
2 · Glue silver braid around both curved edges.
3 · Place around the bottom of an arm overlapping the edges at the back. Glue down. Repeat for the other gauntlet.

SHOULDER STRAPS

1 · Cut two pieces of glittery green braid each 22.5cm (9in) long. Glue silver braid on both edges of each piece.
2 · Glue around the body over the shoulders with the ends meeting at the back and front (Fig 1).

Fig 1

BELT

1 · Cut one from buckram and one slightly bigger from glittery pink fabric.
2 · Make as for the Christmas Fairy.
3 · Glue silver braid around the edge and four shiny beads on the front.

HAIR

Make as for Hairstyle 2 in the Methods section of Chapter 1, using mustard wool.

MASK

Make as for the Diver using silver fabric.

CAPE

1 · Cut a piece of glittery pink fabric, 60cm (23½in) × 20cm (8in) and gather one long edge to fit around the neck.
2 · Make the collar as for the Wizard but use glittery pink fabric to cover the buckram.
3 · Using the collar pattern, cut one from black felt and glue onto the back of the collar.

TRIMMINGS

1 · Trim the neck edge with silver braid.
2 · Glue silver ribbon around the bottom of each boot and up the centre seam. Trim around the top of each boot with silver braid.

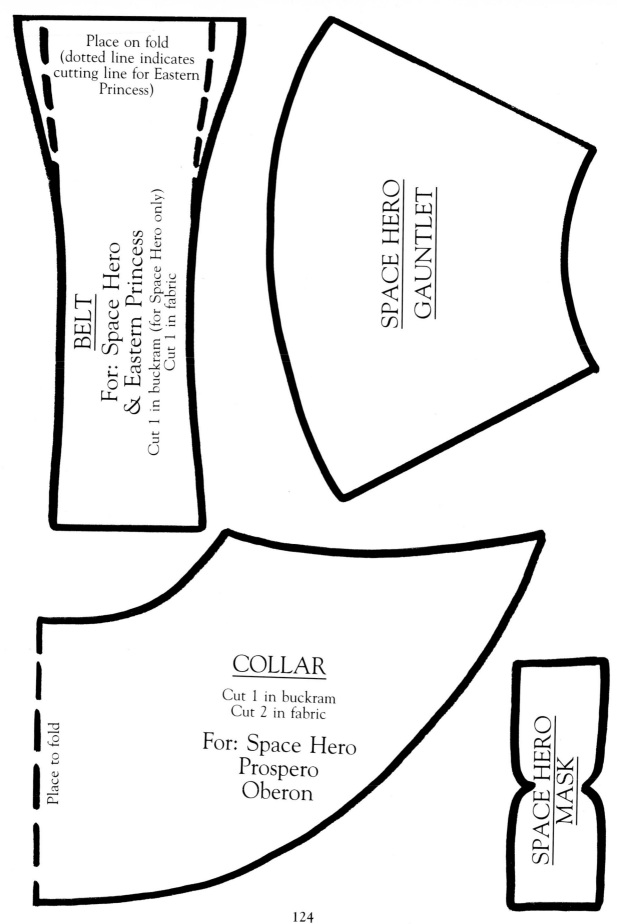

Place on fold
(dotted line indicates
cutting line for Eastern
Princess)

BELT
For: Space Hero
& Eastern Princess
Cut 1 in buckram (for Space Hero only)
Cut 1 in fabric

SPACE HERO
GAUNTLET

Place to fold

COLLAR

Cut 1 in buckram
Cut 2 in fabric

For: Space Hero
Prospero
Oberon

SPACE HERO
MASK

124

Shakespearean Dolls

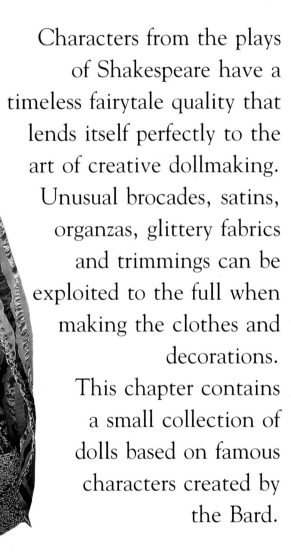

Characters from the plays of Shakespeare have a timeless fairytale quality that lends itself perfectly to the art of creative dollmaking. Unusual brocades, satins, organzas, glittery fabrics and trimmings can be exploited to the full when making the clothes and decorations. This chapter contains a small collection of dolls based on famous characters created by the Bard.

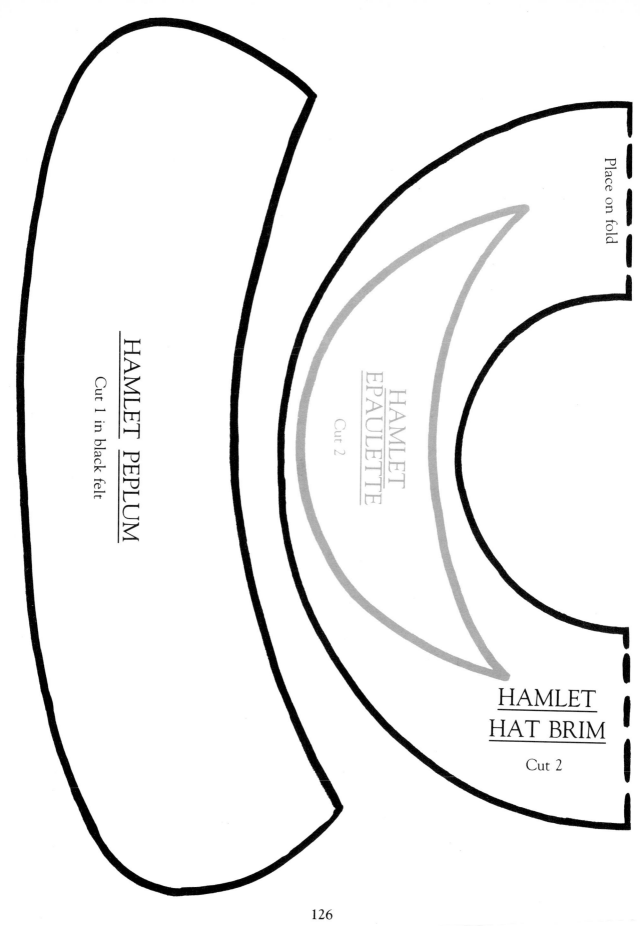

HAMLET PEPLUM

Cut 1 in black felt

HAMLET
EPAULETTE

Cut 2

Place on fold

HAMLET
HAT BRIM

Cut 2

HAMLET

MATERIALS

1m (38in) × 30cm (12in) of black felt for the boots, epaulettes and peplum
35cm (14in) × 25cm (9½in) of black taffeta for the body
1.5m (57in) of black glittery braid
50cm (19½in) of silver ribbon
30cm (12in) of lilac braid
50cm (19½in) square of grey patterned satin for the legs and sleeves
30cm (12in) × 12cm (4in) of white organza for the ruff
56cm (22in) × 20cm (8in) of purple taffeta for the hat
A white feather
Dark yellow textured wool for hair

Use Body Pattern 1. Make the body from black taffeta, the arms from calico, the legs from grey satin and the boots from black felt.

BODY

Using the black glittery braid, glue a 13cm (5½in) piece down the centre front and a piece the same length on either side of the body in a slight curve.

SLEEVES

Make from grey patterned satin in the same way as the Pirate.

EPAULETTES

1 · Cut from black felt and glue four small pieces of black glittery braid across each piece at intervals. Glue the ends over onto the back.
2 · Sew onto the top of each arm as for the Pirate.

PEPLUM

1 · Cut one from black felt using the pattern and glue black glittery braid around all the edges.
2 · Sew onto the bottom of the body with the opening at the front.

RUFF

Make in the same way as for the Elizabethan doll.

HAT

1 · Using the brim pattern, cut two from taffeta and, with right sides facing, sew together around the edge and clip the curves.
2 · Push out through the centre hole and press.
3 · Cut a 9cm (3½in) radius circle of taffeta for the crown. Run a gathering thread around the edge to fit the centre of the brim.

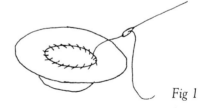

Fig 1

4 · With right sides facing, sew the crown to the centre of the brim (Fig 1).
5 · Sew a white feather onto one side of the hat.

HAIR

Using yellow wool, make as for Oberon (p132). Glue the hat securely onto the head.

TRIMMINGS

1 · Tie a piece of silver ribbon into a bow on each wrist.
2 · Make another bow from silver ribbon and glue onto the centre front of the body.
3 · Glue lilac braid around the top of each boot.

OPHELIA

MATERIALS

1m (38in) × 50cm (19½in) of patterned chiffon for the overskirt and sleeves
1m (38in) × 50cm (19½in) of silver fabric for the body, arms and underskirt
1m (38in) of gathered lace
1m (38in) of silver ribbon
50cm (19½in) of narrow lilac ribbon
23cm (9in) of 5cm (2in) wide grey satin ribbon
4 fabric roses
Lemon textured wool for hair

Use Body Pattern 3. Make the body and arms from silver fabric, the legs from calico and the shoes from felt.

SKIRT

1 · Cut a piece of chiffon 80cm (32in) × 33cm (13in). Hem one long edge and sew gathered lace to this edge. With right sides facing, join the short edges together and then push out to the right side.

2 · For the underskirt, cut a piece of silver fabric 80cm (32in) × 33cm (13in). Hem one long edge and, with right sides facing, sew the short edges together. Push out to the right side.

3 · Fit the chiffon skirt over the silver one with raw edges together, gather through both layers to fit around the waist. Pull up the gathers and fasten off securely.

4 · Cover the waist edge by sewing a piece of wide ribbon around and overlapping the edges at the back and stitching down.

SLEEVES

Make in the same way as the Pirate from chiffon fabric.

HAIR

Using lemon coloured wool make as described for Hairstyle 1 in the Methods section of Chapter 1. Leave the hair long.

TRIMMINGS

1 · Glue a fabric rose onto the bottom of each sleeve.

2 · For the hair decoration, take a few strands of wool on either side of the head and tie with a long piece of silver ribbon. Glue a rose on each side.

3 · Glue a piece of gathered lace around the neck edge. Make a bow from a long piece of narrow lilac ribbon and glue onto the neck to finish.

TITANIA

MATERIALS

90cm (36in) × 50cm (19½in) of glittery green fabric for the underskirt,
upper body and arms
90cm (36in) × 50cm (19½in) of patterned chiffon for the overskirt and puff sleeves
Small length of bright pink organza to trim the waist
30cm (12in) garden stick for the staff
Fabric flowers to decorate the staff, sleeves and headdress
Pink/purple textured wool for hair
10cm (4in) length of silver braid for the neck

Use Body Pattern 1. Make the upper body and arms from green glittery fabric.

SKIRT

1 · Cut a piece of glittery green fabric and a piece of chiffon each 80cm (32in) × 34cm (13½in). Hem one long edge 1cm (½in) on each piece.
2 · With right sides facing, join the short edges on each piece. Push out to the right side.
3 · Fit the glittery green skirt inside the chiffon one and with both long raw edges matching, gather to fit around the waist.
4 · To decorate the waist edge, tie a length of bright pink organza around and secure down at the back with a few stitches.

Fig 1

SLEEVES

1 · Cut six pieces of chiffon, each 25cm (9½in) × 8cm (3in). With right sides facing, join the short edges of each piece and turn out to the right side.
2 · Hem each edge and gather along each edge to fit around the arms. Gather three puff sleeves onto each arm (Fig 1).
3 · Trim each sleeve by sticking on a fabric flower.

HAIR

Make the hair from textured wool as described for Hairstyle 1 in the Methods section of Chapter 1. Leave the hair long.

HEADDRESS AND STAFF

1. · For the headdress, glue fabric flowers and leaves halfway round the head.
2 · For the staff, wrap fabric flowers and leaves spirally around a 30cm (12in) garden stick. Sew securely to one hand.

TRIMMINGS

Sew a length of silver braid around the neck to complete.

OBERON

MATERIALS

1m (38in) × 50cm (19½in) of green satin for the upper body, skirt and puff sleeves
20cm (8in) × 20cm (8in) of silver fabric for arms
1m (38in) × 45cm (17½in) of silver net
30cm (12in) × 15cm (6in) of buckram for the collar
2m (76in) of glittery green braid
50cm (19½in) × 10cm (4in) of green organza for the headdress
30cm (12in) garden stick
50cm (19½in) × 5cm (2in) of darker green organza and pearl beading for the staff
Purple/blue textured wool

Use Body Pattern 1. Make the upper body from green satin and the sleeves from silver fabric.

SKIRT

1 · Cut a piece of green satin 80cm (32in) × 34cm (13½in). Hem one long edge and, with right sides together, join the short edges then turn out to the right side.
2 · Gather the top edge to fit around the waist. Trim the bottom edge of the skirt with glittery green braid.

SLEEVES

1 · Cut four pieces of green satin each 25cm (9½in) × 10cm (4in). Sew the short edges together then turn out to the right side.
2 · Hem both edges on each sleeve and gather the edges to fit onto each arm as for Titania.
3 · Trim the edge of each sleeve with glittery braid.

CAPE

Make in the same way as the Wizard but use silver net for the cape and collar. Trim the edge of the collar with glittery green braid.

HAIR AND BEARD

Make from purple/blue wool in the same way as the Wizard cutting the beard slightly smaller.

HEADDRESS

Ruffle a 50cm (19½in) × 10cm (4in) piece of green organza around the front of the head stitching down here and there.

STAFF

1 · Cover a 30cm (12in) garden stick by wrapping dark green organza around.
2 · Wrap pearl beading spirally around the stick catching down with a few stitches. Sew securely to one hand.

MIRANDA

MATERIALS

90cm (36in) × 50cm (19½in) of blue/purple satin for the upper body, arms and skirt
1m (38in) × 33cm (13in) of glittery blue fabric for the sleeves and underskirt
1m (38in) of 3cm (1in) wide silver braid
2m (76in) of glittery braid
1m (38in) of pale purple braid to trim overskirt
30cm (12in) of purple ribbon to trim the waist
1m (38in) of narrow blue ribbon
50cm (19½in) of narrow green ribbon
30cm (12in) of purple braid to decorate the wrists
Pale blue textured wool for the hair

Use Body Pattern 1. Make the upper body and arms from blue/purple satin.

SKIRT

1 · Cut a 60cm (24in) × 33cm (13in) piece of glittery blue fabric for the underskirt.
2 · Hem one long edge and sew glittery braid to it. With right sides facing, join the short edges and turn out to the right side. Gather the top to fit around the waist and fasten off securely.
3 · Cut a piece of blue/purple satin 80cm (32in) × 33cm (13in) for the overskirt. Hem the two short edges and one long edge 1cm (½in) and sew pale purple braid and then glittery braid to these edges.
4 · Gather the remaining raw edge to fit around the waist leaving the opening at the front.
5 · Cover the waist edge with purple ribbon. Trim each side of the ribbon with glittery braid.

SLEEVES

Make from glittery blue fabric as for the Queen of Hearts.

HAIR

1 · Using blue wool, make as for Hairstyle 1 as described in the Methods section of Chapter 1. Leave the hair long.
2 · Take twelve strands of wool at the front of the head on either side. Make a plait on each side and tie in a bow with narrow green ribbon.
3 · Take a few strands of wool on either side of the top of the head. Tie in a bow with a long length of narrow blue ribbon.

TRIMMINGS

1 · Glue purple braid around each wrist and glittery braid around the neck edge to complete.

PROSPERO

MATERIALS

*90cm (36in) × 50cm (19½in) of blue/gold patterned fabric for the skirt,
upper body and arms
1m (38in) × 45cm (17½in) of shiny striped fabric for the cape
30cm (12in) × 15cm (6in) of buckram for the collar
2m (76in) of glittery blue braid (or a selection of braids, as in the photograph)
2m (76in) of 3cm (1in) wide silver braid
Grey wool for the hair and beard*

Use Body Pattern 1. Make the upper body and arms from blue/gold patterned fabric.

SKIRT
1 · Make as for Oberon using the blue/gold patterned fabric and trimming the bottom with a double layer of wide silver braid.
2 · Glue glittery blue braid around the waist.

CAPE
Using shiny striped fabric, make as for Oberon, trimming the edge of the collar and around the cape with glittery blue braid.

HAIR AND BEARD
Using grey wool make as for Oberon.

TRIMMINGS
1 · Glue a length of glittery blue braid around the head for a headdress.
2 · Glue braid around each wrist to complete.

MACBETH

MATERIALS

90cm (36in) × 50cm (19½in) of glittery purple fabric for the skirt, upper body and arms
1m (38in) × 45cm (17½in) of green satin for the cape
2m (76in) of gold ribbon to trim the bottom of the skirt and wrists
50cm (19½in) of 3cm (1in) wide red/gold braid for the crown and waist decoration
2m (76in) of of wide gold braid to trim the cape
2 large silver buttons and gold ribbon for the shoulder decorations
Rust coloured wool for the hair and beard

Use Body Pattern 1. Make the upper body and arms from glittery purple fabric.

SKIRT
Using glittery purple fabric, make as for Oberon. Sew a double layer of gold ribbon around the bottom edge. Trim the waist edge with red/gold braid.

CAPE
1 · Make as for the Wizard trimming the edge with wide gold braid and omitting the collar.

2 · For the shoulder decorations, gather a piece of gold ribbon into a rosette and glue onto the back of a large silver button. Repeat for the other button and glue both firmly onto the shoulders.

HAIR AND BEARD
Using rust coloured wool, make in the same way as the Wizard.

DECORATIONS
Glue a piece of red/gold braid around the head for a crown.

LADY MACBETH

MATERIALS

90cm (36in) × 50cm (19½in) of red/silver fabric for the skirt, upper body and arms
2m (76in) of red/gold braid to trim the bottom of the skirt, waist and wrists (or two different braids, as in the photograph)
1m (38in) of gold braid
30cm (12in) of gold ribbon
80cm (32in) × 30cm (12in) of non-fray red satin for the cape
Large gold button
Red textured wool for hair

Use Body Pattern 1. Make the upper body and arms from red/silver patterned fabric.

SKIRT

1 · Make as for Oberon trimming the bottom edge with red/gold braid.
2 · Trim the waist edge with red/gold braid.

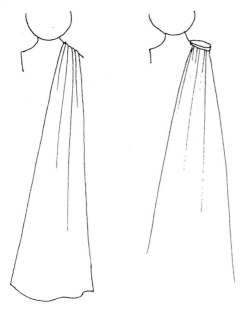

Fig 1   *Fig 2*

SHOULDER CAPE

1 · Cut a piece of non-fray red satin 80cm (32in) × 30cm (12in).
2 · Gather through the middle and then fasten off. Sew to top of one shoulder along the gathered line (Fig 1).
3 · Sew a large gold button on top of the gathers to complete (Fig 2).

HAIR

1 · Using red wool, make as described for Hairstyle 1 in the Methods section of Chapter 1. Leave the hair long.
2 · Take fifteen strands of wool on one side and make a plait. Tie with a piece of gold ribbon.
3 · Glue two strips of gold braid around the head for a headband.

TRIMMINGS

Trim the neck edge with gold braid to complete.

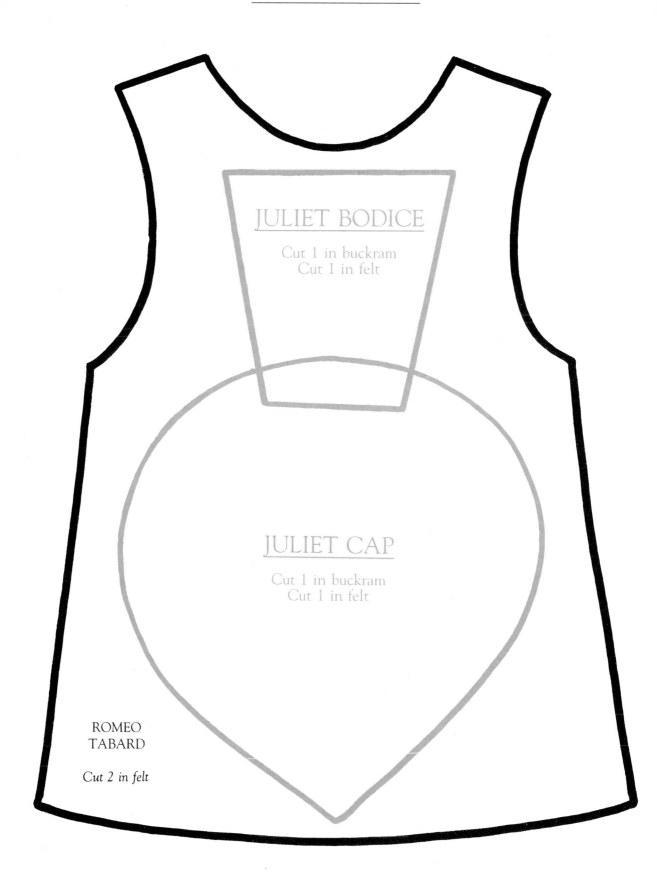

JULIET BODICE

Cut 1 in buckram
Cut 1 in felt

JULIET CAP

Cut 1 in buckram
Cut 1 in felt

ROMEO
TABARD

Cut 2 in felt

JULIET

MATERIALS

90cm (36in) × 50cm (19½in) of dusky pink/lilac satin for the arms, body and underskirt
1m (38in) × 33cm (13in) of dusky pink corduroy for the overskirt and puff sleeves
3m (114in) of patterned ribbon
3m (114in) of gathered lace
Small pieces of glittery braid to decorate the sleeves and neck
4 fabric roses
22cm (8½in) × 15cm (6in) of buckram
23cm (9in) × 16cm (6½in) of pale pink felt
50cm (19½in) of narrow gold braid
33cm (13in) of pink braid
Brown textured wool for the hair

Use Body Pattern 3. Make the arms and body from dusky pink/lilac satin, the legs from flesh calico and the shoes from pink felt.

SKIRT

1 · Using the pink/lilac satin, cut a piece 60cm (24in) × 33cm (13in) for the underskirt. Sew gathered lace to one long edge.
2 · With right sides together, join the short edges and turn out to the right side. Gather around the waist and faten off.
3 · For the overskirt, cut a piece of pink corduroy 60cm (24in) × 33cm (13in) and hem two short edges and one long edge. Sew gathered lace and ribbon to these three edges.
4 · Gather the remaining edge around the waist. Pull the gathers tightly and fasten off. Decorate the waist edge with gathered lace.

BODICE DECORATION

1 · Using the pattern cut one from buckram and one from felt. Glue the felt onto one side of the buckram.
2 · Glue gold braid in a criss-cross pattern on the felt side and then sew gathered lace around the edge.

3 · Glue the bodice decoration onto the front of the doll with the bottom edge just covering the front of the skirt.

SLEEVES

1 · Cut two pieces of corduroy each 22cm (8½in) × 12cm (4½in).
2 · With right sides facing, sew the two short edges together and turn out to the right side.
3 · Turn in the raw edges and gather the top and bottom of both sleeves to fit onto the top of each arm.
4 · Trim the bottom edge of each sleeve with gathered lace, followed by a piece of glittery braid sewn just underneath.
5 · Sew a rose onto the bottom of each sleeve.

HAIR

Using brown textured wool, make as described for Hairstyle 1 in the Methods section of Chapter 1. Leave the hair long.

JULIET CAP

1 · Using the pattern, cut one from buckram. Wet the buckram slightly under running water and mould around a small ball or a piece of fruit

to create a curved shape. Leave to dry.

2 · Cut one from pink felt 2cm (½in) larger all round than the pattern. Sew around the edge of the cap, turning the ends underneath and stitching down.

3 · Decorate the top by sticking on narrow gold braid in a criss-cross pattern. Finish by sticking

pink braid around the edge.

4 · Glue the cap onto the head.

TRIMMINGS

1 · Decorate the neck edge with glittery braid.

2 · To finish the skirt, sew a rose onto both bottom corners.

ROMEO

MATERIALS

80cm (32in) × 50cm (19½in) of shiny checked fabric for the body, arms, legs and sleeves
50cm (19½in) square of light brown felt for the boots and hat
A pink feather
70cm (28in) length of braid for the hat
40cm (15½in) × 22cm (9in) of pale pink felt for the tabard
1m (38in) of glittery rust braid
30cm (12in) length of rust satin ribbon
40cm (15½in) length of gold ribbon
Textured brown wool for hair

Use Body Pattern 3. Make the body, arms and legs from shiny checked fabric and the boots from light brown felt. Before making the head, make the tabard as described below.

TABARD

1 · Using the pattern, cut two from pale pink felt and, with right sides facing, join at the shoulder seams. Press the seams open and turn out to the right side.

2 · Glue or sew glittery rust braid around all the edges including the neck edge.

3 · Place on top of the doll.

4 · Catch the sides together with a few stitches. Now make the head.

SLEEVES

Make in the same way as for the Pirate. Tie the ends with gold ribbon fastening into a bow.

HAIR

Make from brown wool in the same way as for Oberon.

HAT

1 · Cut a 5cm (2in) radius circle and a strip 34cm (13½in) × 4cm (1½in) from light brown felt.

2 · Sew the short edges together and turn out to the right side.

3 · With the right sides facing, slipstitch the strip of felt around the edge of the felt circle. Turn out to the right side.

4 · Sew braid around the top and lower edge of the hat and sew a feather to one side.

5 · With the seam at the back glue the hat on top of the head.

TRIMMINGS

1 · Glue glittery braid around the top of boot.

2 · Make a bow from rust satin ribbon and leave the ends long. Glue to neck edge of tabard.

The Land
of the
Little People

Welcome to a magic kingdom where fairies, pixies, gnomes and leprechauns live in harmony deep in the forest amongst the tree roots and foliage.

The dolls in this chapter are all made using Body Pattern 4. By adding your own individual trimmings and decorations you can soon create your own enchanted kingdom full of little people.

FAIRIES

LILAC FAIRY

MATERIALS

70cm (27½in) × 30cm (12in) of lilac organza
60cm (23½in) × 15cm (6in) of blue net for the underskirt
23cm (9in) × 15cm (6in) of lilac felt for shoes
23cm (9in) × 19cm (7½in) of pink/white dotty fabric
30cm (12in) × 23cm (9in) of lilac satin for the body
15cm (6in) × 4cm (1½in) of blue felt for the neck frill
23cm (9in) × 12cm (5in) of buckram
23cm (9in) × 12cm (5in) of shiny pearlised fabric
5cm (2in) strip of velcro
30cm (12in) of blue braid
9 purchased blue satin rosebuds
2 small toy bells
25cm (10in) of 3cm (1in) wide lilac ribbon
40cm (15½in) of string sequins
Purple wool for hair
20cm (8in) of 3cm (1in) wide silver braid for the crown
30cm (12in) gold pipecleaner and narrow green ribbon for the wand

Use Body Pattern 4. Make the legs from dotty fabric, the shoes from felt and the body from lilac satin.

Sew two eyelashes on each eye instead of three.

SKIRT

1 · Cut a piece of blue net 60cm (23½in) × 15cm (6in) for the underskirt. Run a gathering thread along one long edge and pull up the

gathers to fit around the waist. Fasten off securely.

2 · For the overskirt, cut a piece of lilac organza 60cm (23½in) × 22cm (8½in) and fold in half lengthways so that the width is now 11cm (4in) (Fig 1).

Fig 1

3 · With right sides facing, sew the back seams together and turn out to the right side. Gather the top raw edge to fit around the waist and fasten off securely.

4 · Cover the waist edge with a piece of lilac ribbon overlapping the edges at the back and stitch down. Trim each edge of the ribbon with string sequins.

5 · Gather up the bottom of the overskirt at 7cm (3in) intervals (Fig 2). Sew a rosebud to each gather.

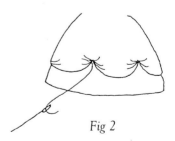

Fig 2

SLEEVES

1 · Cut two pieces of lilac organza each 17cm (6½in) × 8cm (3in).

2 · With right sides facing, join the short edges of each piece and turn out to the right side.

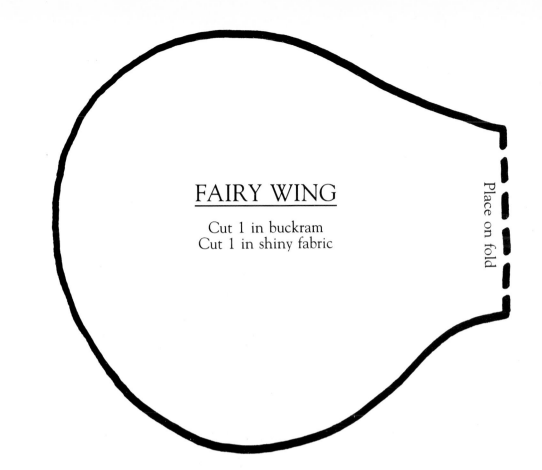

FAIRY WING

Cut 1 in buckram
Cut 1 in shiny fabric

Place on fold

NECK FRILL FOR ALL LITTLE PEOPLE

Cut 1 in felt

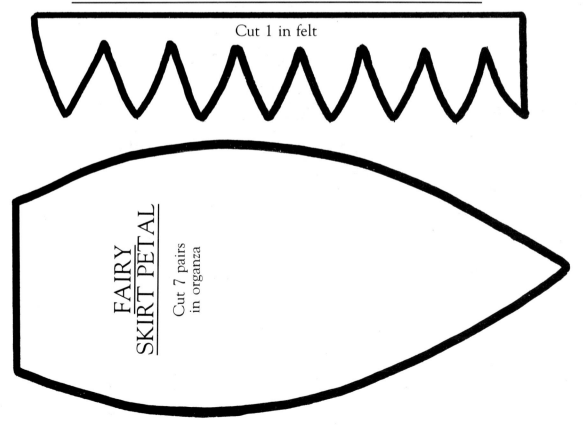

FAIRY SKIRT PETAL

Cut 7 pairs
in organza

3 · Turn in both long edges on each sleeve and gather to fit onto each arm.

WINGS

1 · Using the pattern, cut one from buckram and one from shiny fabric.

2 · Tack the shiny piece on top of the buckram and then stitch around the edge. Remove the tacking stitches.

3 · Cut a strip of velcro 5cm (2in) long and sew one piece down the centre of the wing on the right side. Sew the other piece on the back of the doll.

4 · Attach the wings to the back of the doll.

HAIR

1 · Make the hair as described for Hairstyle 1 in the Methods section of Chapter 1.

2 · Tie the hair into a pony tail at the back and cut off any long strands of wool.

3 · For the crown, cut a 20cm (8in) length of silver braid. Glue the ends together and glue onto the head.

WAND

1 · Bend a 30cm (12in) pipecleaner in half and wrap narrow green ribbon around in a spiral motion securing the ends with a dab of glue.

2 · Sew the wand securely to one hand.

TRIMMINGS

1 · Using the pattern, cut a neck frill from felt and glue around the neck.

2 · Glue blue braid around the top of each shoe and around each sleeve.

3 · Sew a small bell onto each shoe to complete.

APPLE FAIRY

MATERIALS

70cm (27½in) × 30cm (12in) of white organza
60cm (23½in) × 15cm (6in) of green net for the underskirt
23cm (9in) × 15cm (6in) of green felt for shoes
23cm (9in) × 19cm (7½in) of blue/white patterned fabric
30cm (12in) × 23cm (9in) of pale green satin
15cm (6in) × 4cm (1½in) of green felt
23cm (9in) × 12cm (5in) of buckram
23cm (9in) × 12cm (5in) of shiny pearlised fabric
5cm (2in) strip of velcro
30cm (12in) of glittery green braid
30cm (12in) × 20cm (8in) of blue shiny fabric for the waistband and bows
40cm (15½in) of sequin trim
2 small toy bells
Pale green wool for hair
Blue fabric flowers for hair decoration
30cm (12in) glittery silver pipecleaner and narrow lilac ribbon for the wand

Use Body Pattern 4. Make the legs from blue/white patterned fabric, the body from pale green satin and the shoes from green felt.

Sew two eyelashes on each eye instead of three.

SKIRT

1 · Make the underskirt from green net in the same way as the Lilac Fairy.

2 · Cut the overskirt from white organza and make in the same way as the Lilac Fairy.

3 · Trim the waist edge with a 20cm (8in) × 6cm (2½in) strip of shiny blue fabric. Fold over the long edges to meet at the back and place around the waist.

4 · Overlap the ends at the back and stitch down. Glue sequin trim around both edges.

5 · For the bows on the skirt, cut nine pieces of shiny blue fabric each 4cm (1½in) × 3cm (1in). Gather through the middle of each piece and place a small strip of blue fabric around the middle stitching down at the back.

6 · Sew the bows around the skirt.

SLEEVES

Using white organza, make as for the Lilac Fairy.

WINGS
Make as for the Lilac Fairy.

HAIR
1 · Using pale green wool make as for the Lilac Fairy.

2 · Make the bun on top in the same way as described for the Mermaid in Chapter 4.

3 · Decorate the bun by sticking blue fabric flowers around the edge.

WAND
Make the wand in the same way as the Lilac Fairy using a silver pipecleaner and lilac ribbon.

TRIMMINGS
1 · Sew glittery green braid around the sleeves and the top of each shoe.

2 · Cut the neck frill from green felt and glue around the neck.

3 · Sew a bell to the point of each shoe.

RASPBERRY FAIRY

MATERIALS

70cm (27½in) × 32cm (12½in) of dark pink organza

60cm (23½in) × 15cm (6in) of pink net for the underskirt

23cm (9in) × 15cm (6in) of pale blue felt

23cm (9in) × 19cm (7½in) of pink/white striped fabric

30cm (12in) × 23cm (9in) of pink satin for the body

15cm (6in) × 4cm (1½in) of purple felt

23cm (9in) × 12cm (5in) of buckram

23cm (9in) × 12cm (5in) of shiny pearlised fabric

5cm (2in) strip of velcro

30cm (12in) of pink/gold braid

25cm (10in) of 3cm (1in) wide pink satin ribbon for the waistband

40cm (15½in) of pink/white braid

7 large pearl beads

2 toy bells

Deep pink coloured wool for hair

Pink fabric flowers for hair decoration

30cm (12in) glittery silver pipecleaner and narrow blue ribbon for the wand

Use Body Pattern 4. Make the legs from pink/white striped fabric, the body from pink satin and the shoes from pale blue felt.
Sew two eyelashes on each eye instead of three.

SKIRT
1 · Make the underskirt from pink net as for the Lilac Fairy. The overskirt is made up of seven petals. Using the petal pattern, cut fourteen from pink organza and, with right sides facing, sew together in pairs from A–B leaving the top straight edge open.

2 · Clip any curves, turn out and press. Sew the petals around the waist.

3 · Sew a pearl bead to the bottom of each petal.

4 · Sew pink satin ribbon around the waist and pink/white braid to both edges of the ribbon.

SLEEVES
Make as for the Lilac Fairy using pink organza.

WINGS
Make as for the Lilac Fairy.

HAIR
1 · Using deep pink wool, make as described for the Apple Fairy.

2 · Glue pink fabric around the bun.

WAND
Make from a silver pipecleaner and blue ribbon as for the Lilac Fairy.

TRIMMINGS
1 · Sew pink/gold braid around sleeves and top of shoes. Sew a bell to each shoe point.

2 · Cut the neck frill from purple felt and glue around the neck.

ORANGE FAIRY

MATERIALS

70cm (27½in) × 32cm (12½in) of orange organza
60cm (23½in) × 15cm (6in) of orange net
23cm (9in) × 15cm (6in) of yellow felt
23cm (9in) × 19cm (7½in) of striped fabric
30cm (12in) × 23cm (9in) of peach satin for the body
15cm (6in) × 4cm (1½in) of white felt for the neck frill
23cm (9in) × 12cm (5in) of buckram
23cm (9in) × 12cm (5in) of shiny pearlised fabric
5cm (2in) strip of velcro
30cm (12in) of white/gold braid
25cm (10in) × 6cm (2½in) of shiny red fabric for the waistband
40cm (15½in) of sequin trim
7 large pearls
2 toy bells
Peach coloured wool for hair
20cm (8in) of 3cm (1in) wide gold braid for the crown
30cm (12in) gold pipecleaner and narrow pink ribbon for the wand

Use Body Pattern 4. Make the legs from striped fabric, the body from peach satin and the shoes from yellow felt.
Sew two eyelashes on each eye instead of three.

SKIRT

1 · Using orange net, make the underskirt in the same way as the Lilac Fairy.
2 · Make the overskirt from orange organza as for the Raspberry Fairy.
3 · Trim the waist with red shiny fabric as for the Apple Fairy. Trim the edges with sequin trim.

SLEEVES

Make in orange organza in the same way as the Lilac Fairy.

WINGS

Make as for the Lilac Fairy.

HAIR

1 · Make from peach wool as for the Lilac Fairy.
2 · For the crown, cut a 20cm (8in) piece of 3cm (1in) wide gold braid. Overlap the back edges and glue down onto the head.

WAND

Make from a gold pipecleaner and wrap narrow pink ribbon around.

TRIMMINGS

1 · Glue white/gold braid around each sleeve and on the top of each shoe.
2 · Cut the neck frill from white felt and glue around the neck.
3 · Sew a bell to the point of each shoe.

GNOMES

MATERIALS

30cm (12in) × 23cm (9in) of fabric for the body
23cm (9in) × 19cm (7½in) of fabric for legs
32cm (12½in) × 24cm (9½in) of felt for boots
2 toy bells
15cm (6in) × 4cm (1½in) of felt for neck frill
40cm (15½in) × 25cm (10in) of satin for sleeves
50cm (19½in) length of silver ribbon
30cm (12in) × 15cm (6in) of felt for the peplum
Small buckle
Piece of felt wide enough to fit through the buckle and 25cm (10in) long
32cm (12½in) × 25cm (10in) of felt for the hat
Small white pompon
25cm (10in) of braid to trim hat
Scrap of white felt for moustache
10cm (4in) × 7cm (3in) of polyester wadding or cotton wool for beard

Use Body Pattern 4. Both gnomes are made in the same way; make the body and legs from striped or dotty fabric and the boots from red or green felt.

Before sewing the legs to the body fit the boot trims as described below.

BOOT TRIMS

1 · Cut two pieces of felt each 13cm (7½in) × 4cm (1½in).
2 · With right sides facing, join the short edges.
3 · With right sides facing, slip over each leg with the bottom level with the boot seam (Fig 1).

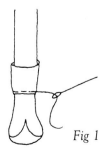

Fig 1

4 · Stitch all the way round through each leg.
5 · Roll the felt over so that the boot trims are now complete (Fig 2). Sew the legs to the body.

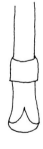

Fig 2

SLEEVES

1 · Make as for the Pirate using satin.
2 · Tie a length of silver ribbon in a bow on each wrist.

PEPLUM

Cut one from felt and glue around the bottom of the body.

BELT

1 · Cut a length of felt 25cm (10in) long and wide enough to fit through the buckle.
2 · Sew one end of the belt to the buckle and fasten around the waist tucking in the ends.

NECK FRILL

Cut from felt and glue securely around the neck.

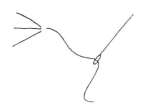

Fig 3

FACE

1 · Instead of black felt eyes, use black thread and sew three stitches in a point on either side of the nose to give a chuckling expression (Fig 3).
2 · Using the pattern, cut a moustache from white felt and a beard from wadding or cotton wool.
3 · Glue the beard just under the nose and the moustache on top.

HAT

1 · Using the Pierrot hat pattern, cut twice in felt and sew together along both long edges.
2 · Turn out to the right side and glue onto the head.
3 · Sew braid around the edge.
4 · Fold the pointed end over at a slight angle and either glue or catch down with a few stitches.
5 · Glue a small pompon to the end to complete.

LEPRECHAUNS

MATERIALS

30cm (12in) × 23cm (9in) of fabric for the body
23cm (9in) × 19cm (7½in) of fabric for the legs
32cm (12½in) × 24cm (9½in) of felt for the boots
30cm (12in) × 15cm (6in) of felt for peplum
2 small buckles
25cm (10in) length of felt wide enough to fit through the buckle at the waist
40cm (15½in) × 25cm (10in) of shiny fabric for sleeves
Narrow green ribbon to tie sleeves
Green or mustard wool for hair
Scrap of white felt for moustache
10cm (4in) × 7cm (3in) of polyester wadding or cotton wool for beard
15cm (6in) × 4cm (1½in) of felt for neck frill
35cm (14in × 26cm (10½in) of green felt for hat
17cm (6½in) square of card
Small amount of toy stuffing
27cm (10½in) piece of felt wide enough to fit through a buckle on the hat
65cm (25½in) of braid or sequin trim to decorate hat

Use Body Pattern 4. Both Leprechauns are made in the same way; use green fabric for the body, green shiny fabric for the legs and felt for the boots. The eyes are sewn in black thread as for the Pixies and Gnomes.

Make the boots in the same way as the Gnomes. Make the peplum, belt, neck frill, sleeves, moustache and beard as for the Gnomes choosing dominantly green fabrics. Tie the bottom of each sleeve with narrow green ribbon.

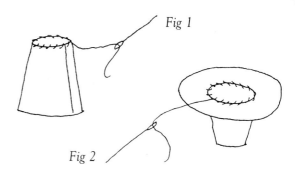

Fig 1

Fig 2

HAIR

Using Green or mustard wool, make as described for Hairstyle 1 in the Methods section of Chapter 1 cutting the hair to shoulder length.

HAT

1 · Using the brim pattern, cut two from felt and one from card. Spread a small amount of glue on either side of the card and sandwich it inbetween the two felt pieces.

2 · Stitch around the inner and outer circles of the brim to secure.

3 · Cut a side piece from felt using the pattern and, with right sides facing, overlap the ends and topstitch.

4 · Cut a crown piece from felt and oversew the crown to the top of the side piece (Fig 1).

5 · Turn out to the right side and oversew the bottom of the side to the inner edge of the brim (Fig 2).

6 · Sew braid or sequin trim around the top of the hat and around the brim.

7 · Cut a 27cm (10½in) strip of felt wide enough to fit through a buckle. With the buckle at the front of the hat sew around the edge overlapping the ends at the back. Insert a small amount of stuffing and glue the hat securely on the head.

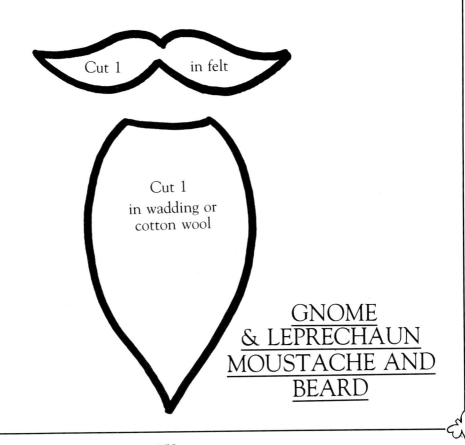

Cut 1   in felt

Cut 1
in wadding or
cotton wool

GNOME & LEPRECHAUN MOUSTACHE AND BEARD

LEPRECHAUN HAT SIDE

Cut 1 in felt

Place on fold

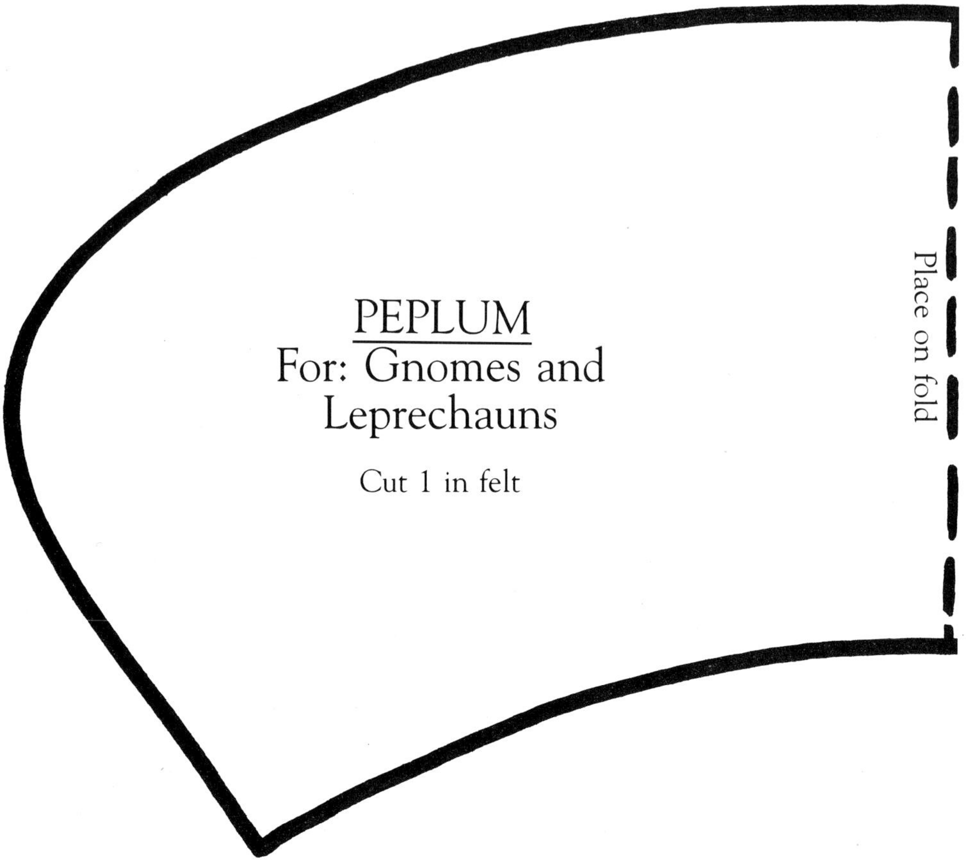

PEPLUM
For: Gnomes and Leprechauns

Cut 1 in felt

Place on fold

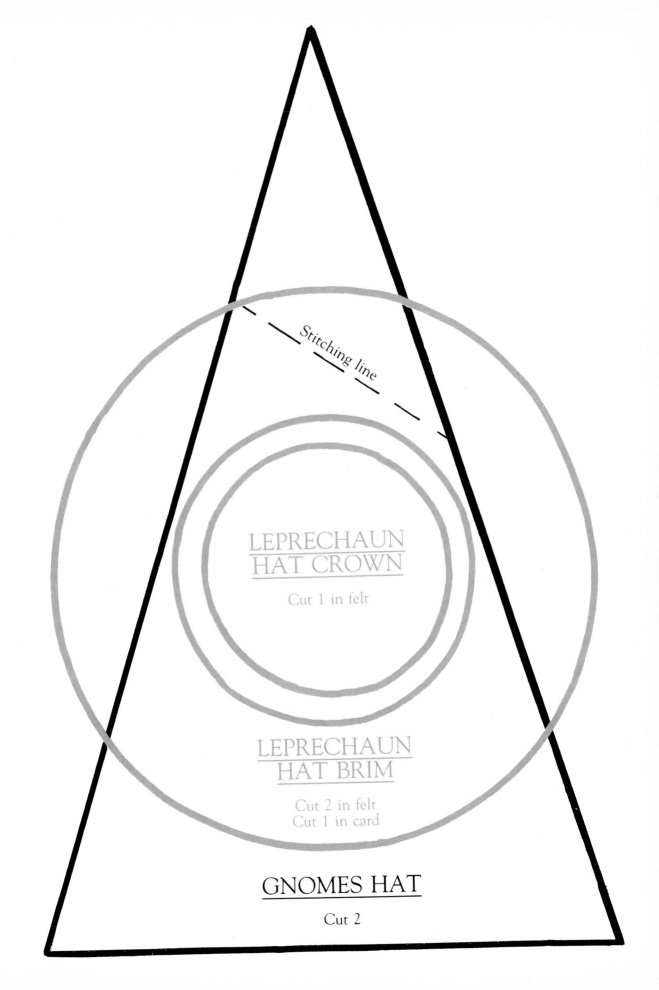

Stitching line

LEPRECHAUN
HAT CROWN

Cut 1 in felt

LEPRECHAUN
HAT BRIM

Cut 2 in felt
Cut 1 in card

GNOMES HAT

Cut 2

PIXIES

MATERIALS

30cm (12in) × 23cm (9in) of fabric for the body
23cm (9in) × 19cm (7½in) of fabric for the legs
23cm (9in) × 15cm (6in) of felt for shoes
20cm (8in) of glittery braid for shoes
2 toy bells
15cm (6in) × 4cm (1½in) of felt for neck frill
55cm (21½in) × 10cm (4in) or organza for waist and arm ruffles
Small scraps of contrasting organza
20cm (8in) × 8cm (3in) of contrast organza for rosebud
Bright coloured wool for hair
25cm (10in) of glittery braid for headband
Two 7cm (2½in) squares of felt for flower in hair

Use Body Pattern 4. Both Pixies are made in the same way; make the body from shiny fabric, the legs from striped or spotty fabric and the shoes from bright coloured felt.

Instead of felt eyes make the eyes in the same way as the Gnomes.

WAIST RUFFLE

1 · Cut a piece of organza 25cm (10in) × 8cm (3in) and gather at 6cm (2½in) intervals.

2 · Cover the gathers with small strips of organza in a contrasting colour and sew the ruffled piece around the waist, overlapping the edges at the back and stitching down.

ARM RUFFLES

1 · Cut two 15cm (6in) × 5cm (2in) strips of organza and gather at 2cm (1in) intervals. Cover with small strips of organza in a contrasting colour.

2 · Sew a ruffled strip around each armhole.

ROSEBUD

1 · Cut a piece of organza 20cm (8in) × 8cm (3in).

2 · Fold in half along the length and then roll up into a rose shape securing with a few stitches at the base.

3 · Sew the rosebud to one side of the waist.

HAIR

Using bright coloured wool, make as described for Hairstyle 1 in the Methods section of Chapter 1 and cut short to shoulder length.

HEADBAND

1 · Glue a 25cm (10in) length of glittery braid around the head.

2 · Using the flower pattern, cut two from different coloured felt.

3 · Place one flower on top of the other and pinch together in the middle securing with a few stitches. Sew securely onto one side of the headband.

TRIMMINGS

1 · Using the pattern, cut a neck frill in bright coloured felt and glue around the neck.

2 · Sew glittery braid around the top of each shoe.

3 · Sew a small bell to the point of each shoe.

INDEX

Numbers in italics indicate illustrations